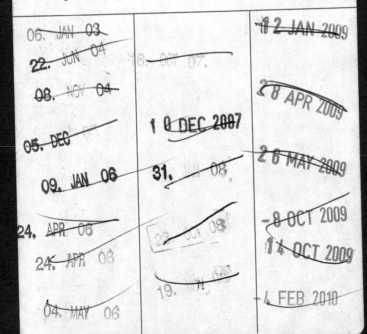

Oscar

© 2002 Assouline Publishing, Inc.

Assouline Publishing, Inc.
601 West 26th Street
18th floor
New York, NY 10001
USA
Tel: 212 989-6810   Fax: 212 647-0005

www.assouline.com

ISBN: 2 84323 343 7

Color separation: Gravor (Switzerland)
Printing: Musumeci (Italy)

Copyedited by Margaret Burnham.

SARAH MOWER

Oscar

THE STYLE, INSPIRATION AND LIFE OF OSCAR DE LA RENTA

FOREWORD BY ANNA WINTOUR

ASSOULINE

Contents

FOREWORD

the fashion industry is, for better or worse, devoted to the generation of illusions: of youth, wealth, and well-being, of the notion that life can be sunny and glamorous around the clock. Oscar de la Renta's exceptional body of work is, in this sense, no exception. Who can look at his fabulously ruffled flamenco dresses without mentally zooming off to a floodlit fiesta by some tropical pool? Who can slip on one of his fur-trimmed double-face suits for Balmain haute couture without fantasizing about hurrying across the Tuileries on a mysterious romantic assignment? But what's wonderful and exceptional about Oscar is that he miraculously embodies and inhabits the fantastic world suggested by his creations. He is a great tennis player, a political mediator, a philanthropist, a society dazzler, a patron of the arts, a diplomat, a devoted family man, and a great designer. I regard him as fashion's Renaissance man.

It has to be acknowledged that Oscar and I got off to a rather rocky start. We met when I was the editor of *House & Garden*, a magazine that I quickly remade and renamed *HG*. I suspect that Oscar looked upon these developments with horror, as if they represented an attack on all that was classy and chic. Nonetheless, before long we were friends, which, as any of his friends will tell you, is a never-ending course in loyalty and generosity and charm. By "his friends," I don't mean simply the names from the society pages. It's true that to have dinner with Oscar at his home in Santo Domingo means breaking bread with Hillary Clinton, Julio Iglesias or the Kissingers, who are all at their most relaxed and most fun in his company. (There is invariably a moment after dinner when Oscar gets to his feet and breaks into song or leads his guests onto the dance floor in a sophisticated merengue. This is quintessential Oscar—hospitable, winning, fearless.) But the most telling moment of the night for me comes after all the celebrities have gone to bed, when Oscar may be found in the kitchen slapping down dominoes with a substantial portion of the population of the Dominican Republic. However much as he loves the company of famously inspiring people, he is equally inspired by the company of the not-so-famous. He considers all of his guests—be it the ex-First Lady or his cook's visiting cousin—to be part of his large, extended family. Oscar is the opposite of a snob: a man of profound humanity.

As a man in love with both the Dominican Republic, his homeland, and New York, his adopted home, Oscar is a tireless champion of such causes as The Met, Carnegie Hall, Channel 13, New Yorkers for Children, the Americas Society and the Spanish Institute. He is the founder of La Casa del Niño, an orphanage and day-care center in the Dominican Republic that provides assistance to over 1,200 children. In Santo Domingo, Oscar's guests may be pressed into service at the orphanage handing out gifts, and may also have the pleasure of visiting the local school, where Oscar knows every teacher's name and background. He is an inspiring figure, one of the few who throws the world into relief in a way that makes moral and aesthetic sense. There is nothing minimal about him—his clothes, his generosity, his parenting (to his son and stepchildren).

It wouldn't be right to praise Oscar without mentioning Annette, his extraordinary wife. She is the dazzling, tireless, and dynamic force that inspires and encourages him in all that he does. We are lucky to have him, and her. This book helps us to understand why.

Anna Wintour

Stories from Oscar de la Renta's childhood read like detailed, fantastical vignettes from Gabriel García Márquez or a highly colored painting by Diego Rivera. Born into a huge, lively, extended family in the tropical sunshine and Latin American culture of the Dominican Republic of the 1930s, he was a much doted-on boy mostly surrounded by women. In the background: exuberant vegetation, passionate romance, and the steamy repressions of a poor Catholic country laboring under a military dictatorship. In the foreground: the whirl and laughter of a happy home inhabited by an adored mother and six sisters. Oscar's father, Oscar de la Renta senior, had an insurance business, but since he had come from Puerto Rico, it was the Dominican side of the family—mother, grandmother, aunts, uncles, cousins, nephews, and nieces—who dominated the daily lives of little Oscar and his sisters.

Oscar de la Renta's grandfather's home in southern Puerto Rico.

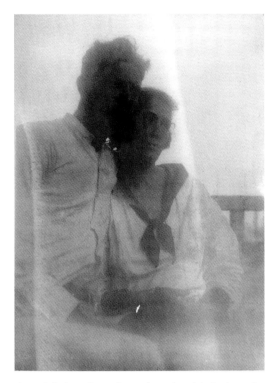

Oscar's father, Oscar Sr., and mother, Maria Antonia.

after more than two hundred years on the island, Maria Antonia's family, the Fiallos, were so embedded in Dominican society that they could count poets, scholars, and businessmen as well as top army brass among their number. The de la Rentas lived in the old city, the Ciudad Colonial, in the capital, Santo Domingo, on a street with a jumble of houses painted pastel blue, canary yellow, and pink. It seemed there were Fiallos, people married to Fiallos, and Fiallo children everywhere, every one of them living in righteous awe of the formidable matriarch, grandmother Juana Fiallo.

Oscar de la Renta's grandmother was slim and upright, and dressed strictly, every day, in long, starched, flounced and ruffled white dresses, with two solitary diamonds in her ears—a visual personification of crisp, disciplined, feminine power that has influenced her grandson's imagination ever since. The remarkable Juana Fiallo, who was born a Perez, had come to the

island from the neighboring island of Curaçao, and raised nine children, dictating the running of family affairs, relationships, and finances down to every last household purchase of fruit till the day she died. So strong was her influence that she managed to repel the attentions of three of her daughters' suitors so effectively (the men, of course, were never good enough) that the girls never married. Even in their sixties, these aunts were so bossed-about they had to ask their mother's permission to entertain female visitors.

Maria Antonia, Juana's fourth daughter, however, somehow managed to gain approval to marry the suavely handsome Oscar de la Renta. Five daughters later, Maria found herself pregnant again. This time, however, she was convinced a much longed-for boy was on the way. It was 1932. Two years earlier, after years of political infighting, the Dominican Republic had fallen under the ruthless military dictatorship of Rafael Trujillo. One of Maria's brothers, Federico, was

Oscar de la Renta Sr.

head of the armed forces under Trujillo, and drove around in a massive car emblazoned with three stars to prove it. Another, Aristedes, was an intellectual—a doctor, lawyer, architect, and recipient of every degree the University of Santo Domingo could confer. Both uncles, one way or another, were to play crucial parts in the drama of their new nephew's earliest years.

There must have been great rejoicing at your birth—a son after so many girls?

I was born a huge boy, 10 pounds, and was christened Oscar Aristedes de la Renta. My second name comes from my uncle, who saved my mother's life, and mine, even before I was born. She had come down with appendicitis and the doctors wanted to operate, though she'd lose the baby. My mother wanted her brother, Aristedes, who was out of the country, to be sent for, against the wishes of the doctors, who were afraid it was too dangerous to wait. In pain and with a fever, she still insisted, saying it was her risk. When the brother arrived at our house, he examined her, sent to the pharmacy, made up a paste to put on her stomach, and in twenty-four hours the fever began to subside. So that's why Aristedes is my middle name. At any rate, that's the story I was always told.

How was your family's life in Santo Domingo in the 1930s?

The Dominican Republic is a tropical country, so I remember color, flowers, sunshine. Wherever I am, I cannot bear to be without sunlight to this day—sunrise is magical to me. When I was little, we had a house in the center of the old town of Santo Domingo, which is one of the oldest cities in the New World, the capital of the first island to be colonized by Christopher Columbus in 1492. We're proud of that. We had a house a block away from the seashore. All my mother's family lived in the same neighborhood. It was an intimate, sheltered life. We had a patio at the back of the house, which my mother divided into plots for all the children to do what they wanted with. I used to grow corn and spinach—which grew incredibly fast—so I could sell them to my mother.

So your love of gardens and nature began then?

I loved the huge mango tree in our garden, and the hibiscus, and the tuberose. There was a ylang-ylang tree in the square, and when it bloomed you could smell it for blocks and blocks at night. Every time I smell it, I'm back there—smell has the longest recall of all the senses. When I made my first perfume in 1977, I asked the perfumer to put ylang-ylang in the formula. And I had a glass dewdrop put on the top of the stopper, because when I was really small I had this idea that if I could get up early enough, I could bottle the dewdrops and sell it as perfume.

As a boy, were you ever aware that there was such a thing as fashion?

Compared to Santo Domingo, Havana was a great, cosmopolitan city, full of Americans and sugar-rich families, and much more advanced than anything in the Dominican Republic. I never went, but my mother loved to go shopping there, and to visit her brother, Fabio Fiallo, the poet, who lived in Cuba. When I asked her why she thought it was the best place on earth, she said, because of *La alegria de el cubano*, the "gaiety of the people." She'd describe her favorite department store, El Encanto, where they sold Christian Dior dresses. She'd buy all my clothes there, unfortunately. She'd bring back these short, very wide-cut pants, and

I was tall with very skinny legs. She made me wear them till the age of seven or eight, when everyone else was in long pants. I'd beg her to buy me long trousers, "a man's suit," because the kids at school called me "Stork Legs."

Did you ever see wonderfully dressed women? Anything that can account for your having become a fashion designer?

Well, when I was seven, my older sister had married and had had a baby, and I was given permission to visit them after school, about four blocks away from our house. I was so proud to be an uncle! Often, on the way, I'd notice the car of my uncle Federico, who was head of the armed forces at the time, parked on a side street. One day I saw him walking toward one of the houses on the street. After that, I'd try to peek into the house on the way to my sister's. Then one day, an unbelievably beautiful blonde woman walked onto the balcony. She was tall, slim, with very white skin and big blue eyes like swimming pools, and was wearing some wonderful sensuous filmy dress. She asked me what I was looking for, and when I said I'd seen my uncle's car parked there, she invited me in, and offered me tea from a samovar. A samovar! She gave me cookies, and when I was leaving, 25 cents, which was a fortune to me. She told me she was a friend of my uncle, and asked me if I would like to be her friend, too. But it would have to be a secret. She was Russian, and her name was Elena. From then on, I went to her house almost every day.

What was a creature like that doing in Santo Domingo?

She'd come to the Dominican Republic as part of an equestrian show made up of former members of the Russian Imperial Guard. She was the wife of an officer, and I saw photographs of her riding full gallop next to her husband, with their son riding with one foot on her shoulder and one on his father's. My uncle had seen the show and fallen madly in love with her, and she became his mistress, and when the time came for the troupe to leave, she stayed on with her son.

And this relationship was incredibly illicit?

It was a Catholic country. Divorce didn't exist in the Dominican Republic at the time, and my uncle was married with children. I didn't understand any of this. But I suppose I too fell in love with the Russian lady. She'd tell me incredible, magical stories about Russia and traveling through Europe, stories that fed my imagination and made me dream. Then, when I was ten, I was found out. One day, I was stung by a swarm of wasps, and came down with a fever. In my delirium, they were trying to feed me, and I was raving, "No, no, I want cookies from the Russian lady!" When I recovered, my mother asked me, "What's this about a Russian lady?" So I told her, but not how often I'd visit her, because I knew there was something not right.

Were you reprimanded?

Not at all. My mother wrote to Elena and said I was recovering from an illness and would she like to come and see me? The family knew of her. So Elena came, met my mother and grandmother, and that's how she entered our life. I was the go-between. Later, I would even have to take my grandmother to lunch every Wednesday to visit Elena and my uncle at the house he had built for her on the outskirts of the city. She'd named it "Vladikafkas" after her hometown in the Caucasus. It was always a big mystery among my classmates that this huge car with the stars on it would draw up and collect me from school early every week. And—it makes me laugh to think about it—one of my duties during these visits was that I would always have to help

On the northeast coast of the Dominican Republic, a wild and deserted beach in El Limon.

my grandmother to the bathroom at some point. She would sit there, surrounded by all her white ruffles and flounces, looking like a swan. A vision! But, of course, I wasn't meant to look.

Do you have any memory of the political situation in the country at that time?

I was brought up in a police state. Some of my family agreed with Trujillo's regime; others were in the opposition. I remember one thing that made an impression on me. My mother began to suffer from multiple sclerosis, and one of the few things she could enjoy in life was playing cards. Every single night she'd play poker with her friends. But gambling was illegal, in case it could be used as a cover for political meetings. It was embarrassing for my uncle that in his own city, a small place, his own sister was breaking the law, when other people had been detained for it. He'd come to the house to remonstrate with her, and threaten to send the police—and she'd say "Fine! As long as you take the table and the cards with us!" One night, I remember a lady diving into my bed when they heard *la perrera*—the police car—come round the streets, because they thought they were going to be arrested. Poker was the only thing that gave my mother pleasure. That, and going to church every single day.

What became of your uncle and Elena?

Their love affair continued passionately into their old age. But when Trujillo was assassinated in 1962, they came to take my uncle away for interrogation, although he had retired. One of his nephews, Viriato Fiallo, was the head of the opposition party. When the police came to his house, they let him go upstairs to get changed. He took a gun and shot himself. Four days later, Elena died of sorrow in her bed.

What were the formative influences in your education?

From the ages of eight to thirteen, I was an altar boy at the church of Our Lady of Las Mercedes—a

On the northeast coast of the Dominican Republic, a wild and deserted beach in El Limon.

beautiful and historical church where the 16th-century monk Lope de Vega wrote part of *Don Juan Tenorio*. The priest, Fray Fidel de Villanueva, a Franciscan, was from a town in Andalusia in Spain and a very influential man in my life, like a father to me. He was the first person who bought me colors to paint, because he always saw me doodling when I was very young. He took me to the art school in Santo Domingo—the national art school, which was right next door to the church.

Was it approved of that you should study art?

My mother always said that she would support me in anything, so long as I was serious about it. Because of her, I was able to go to art school. My father was never interested in my artistic career, because he'd built up his business and I was the only son who might one day take over. But I started at the art school in 1946, very early, at the age of fourteen, so I was five years younger than my peers. I'd go to high school from eight to one, and then to art school from two till seven in the evening. I was really lucky, because the school was at its

Oscar's father with his daughter Giorgiana.

height then. Because of the Spanish Civil War, when so many creative people had had to emigrate, we had extraordinary teachers: José Gausachs, José Vela Zanetti, Domingo Pascual. Today, most Dominican kids who can afford to go to school abroad would be sent to the United States, but in my time we thought of Spain as the motherland, and when I graduated, that is where I thought of going.

How did you come to leave home?

I wanted to go to Spain. My closest friend from art school, Fernando Peña Defillo, had left a year earlier to study at the San Fernando art school in Madrid. It wouldn't be too difficult: I spoke the language, the Dominican ambassador to Spain was a cousin of my mother's, and she could fix up a family for me to stay with. So it was decided I could go. Tragically, my mother died of her illness when I was eighteen. The following year, I left on the boat for Spain.

Oscar holding his first nephew, Elio Augusto, with his sisters Avelina (top right) and Alicia (bottom right), with friends from the neighborhood.

OPPOSITE: Oscar as a teenager in Santo Domingo.

After twenty-eight days of relentless seasickness on board a Spanish passenger ship on a stormy winter Atlantic, Oscar de la Renta landed, gratefully, in Madrid in January 1952. He was nineteen, tall, dark, good-looking, and talented—but an ingenue. In spite of having had a one-man show of his landscape paintings back in Santo Domingo, Oscar de la Renta had never been abroad, or apart from his family, in his life. He arrived, full of anticipation, to attend the Real Academia de Bellas Artes de San Fernando. It was a freezing winter and he was to lodge in a family-run pension with four other students. Carrying in his luggage what he thought was the appropriate "artistic" wardrobe—including navy blue suede shoes and a painter's beret—he was lonely at first, missing the mother he had lost, and shocked to be living in a house that had a bathroom with no hot running water. "Are you sick that you have to bathe every day?" asked the landlady.

TOP: Flamenco was a formative influence on Oscar in Spain. The style is reflected here in this printed organza dress from the Spring collection 2001.

BOTTOM: "It was an unbelievable revelation...Pilar Lopez wearing a cobalt flamenco dress." Oscar witnessed Flamenco star Pilar Lopez dancing on the night of his arrival in Spain.

"The good manners, the charm, that fantastic Latin quality he focuses on you make you feel you've suddenly turned into a combination of Sophia Loren and Grace Kelly. He always wants you to look good in his clothes, not the clothes to look good on you. Oscar will say 'no' to the most expensive or fanciest piece you've chosen if he thinks it doesn't show you off well. Since he has such a great eye for line and impact, you will always look your best for men and women."

Barbara Black

Poster advertising a dance concert featuring Pilar Lopez.

The splendor of a bull-fighter's costume is feminized in a tulle blouse and wool embroidered jacket for Balmain, Winter 2001.

althought General Franco was in power, the Spain of the early 1950s was to Oscar's eyes a pleasure dome, a playground of sophistication compared to the secure but sheltered life he had led in the Dominican Republic. He was electrified by this sudden exposure to the sights, sounds, and drama of the roots of his Spanish culture. The emotional impact of seeing art treasures, bullfights, flamenco, and Gypsy culture in the raw burned itself on his receptive visual imagination, crystallizing his taste in a way that would shape his later work forever after. He used his spare time to travel around Spain and see and experience all he could of a country that was still divided along ancient lines—aristocracy on the one hand, peasants and Gypsies on the other.

Meanwhile, the youth seized his opportunities. Blessed with an innate social ease and deliriously in charge of his own freedom for the first time, he grabbed life with both hands, moving effortlessly into the vibrant social scene of Madrid, where artists and aristocracy freely mixed. A charming, well-mannered and well-brought-up youth, he instantly made well-connected friends and learned how to polish his appearance to the almost impossibly glossy standards of gentlemanly correctness and elegance that prevailed among his new European peer group. But as Oscar settled into late Spanish hours and the leisurely pace of an old-world, upper-class way of living, his attendance at art school dropped off. Finally, it was his scrutiny of every last captivating detail of the ways of well-dressed women that eventually distracted Oscar de la Renta from his studies. Thus, though he never guessed it at the time, his fate and fortune were sealed.

The Spain he had arrived in was, after all, no provincial fashion backwater. Cristobal Balenciaga, arguably the finest and most original 20th-century couturier, was a Spaniard, born in San Sebastian. By the mid-1950s, Balenciaga was at the height of his powers, with an awesomely thriving fashion house in Paris and two more haute couture establishments at home—one in Barcelona, the other in Madrid. There is no contemporary comparison for the influence Balenciaga wielded at the time, and certainly no parallel anywhere for the publicity-shunning secrecy with which he shrouded his work. With his meticulous and revolutionary designs, as well as the cloak of privacy he threw over his house, he attracted the clientele he deserved: women of the utmost discretion and discrimination, with a desire for an esthetic elevated somewhere far above the flashiness of obvious wealth. As Diana Vreeland put it in her book *DV*, "A woman dressed by Balenciaga in the fifties and sixties walked into a room and had a dignity, an authority, a thing beyond a question of taste."

"Oscar's designs were always much more European, feminine and always with a touch of Spanish," says his long-time friend Mica Ertegun.

LEFT: Stella Tennant, a bride in satin printed dress, Balmain, Winter 2001.

OPPOSITE: Cascades of taffeta ruffles for Oscar de la Renta, Fall 2001.

Balenciaga wasn't the only fashion presence in Oscar de la Renta's adopted home, though. Such was the fashion system in those days that the city supported numerous houses and tailors who worked flat out to keep well-to-do ladies in the elaborate made-to-measure wardrobes needed for their leisurely lifestyles. Ready-to-wear scarcely existed, and the entire world of fashion spun around the rituals of haute couture. It was into the fringes of this enchanted, extravagant world that the urbane, quick-witted, and sharp-eyed Oscar de la Renta found himself being increasingly, and decisively, drawn.

LEFT: A pleated one-shoulder dress for Balmain, Spring 1998.

CENTER TOP: Christy Turlington, Iman, and Linda Evangelista in printed taffeta dresses for Spring 1988.

CENTER BOTTOM:
Oscar dancing with La Chunga, a star of fla-menco, in Madrid in the 1990s.

RIGHT: Drawing of two sevillanas, 19th century.

66 Charming is applicable to him and his clothes...his things have a chic-a-boom and bounce, they have the sun in them. 99

John Fairchild

"He likes that extra ruffle. That extra print. His clothes are joyous, the way he is," says Anna Wintour.

LEFT: A silk organza ruffled halter, Spring 1973 collection.

RIGHT: The exuberance of the dance captured in a crystal-pleated skirt with wrap halter in 2001.

Oscar de la Renta learned the fundamentals of couture while working for Christobal Balenciaga, photographed here in 1927.

What were your first impressions of Spain when you arrived in 1951?

The very first night I arrived, my friend Fernando Peña Defillo had bought us tickets to go see a famous dancer, Pilar Lopez, who had a company that performed traditional Spanish dance. It was classic Spanish dancing of the eighteenth century, like you see in Goya paintings and flamenco: *ballet clásico español*. That was an unbelievable revelation, something I'll always remember. That night was the premiere of a ballet set to the *Concierto de Aranjuez*, which is about light, and whose composer, Joaquín Rodrigo, was blind. I remember Pilar Lopez in the "night" movement, the only woman among six men, and how she suddenly appeared wearing a cobalt blue flamenco dress—the *bata de cola*—with the ruffles and a long train, and an emerald green shawl thrown across her. I see the whole thing now as vividly as at that moment.

You were only nineteen, and suddenly experiencing the cultured, sophisticated life of Madrid. How did you react?

I'd lived such a restricted life in the Dominican Republic, I was so naïve, you can't imagine. After seeing Pilar Lopez, I was mad about flamenco music. So I became friends with all the dancers and singers, and entangled in the flamenco world that revolved around the Café Villa Rosa. But I had so much to learn. At art school, I met a son of a grand Spanish family, Fernando Valdemar, who'd been educated in England. He took one look at me, with my navy blue suede shoes, and said, "I'd better teach you how to dress." He took me to his tailor. At that time, you could have a custom-made suit for $8, and my father was sending me $125 a month from home, which was a lot in Spain. So practically every afternoon I'd go to the tailor, and in that way, I picked up a lot about how clothes should be fitted. Quickly, I became a señorito—an upper-class dandy, with my custom-made suit, high starched collars, and always a red carnation in my buttonhole. But it had to be the right red: only very, very dark would do. To this day, I still order my suits from the same tailor in Madrid, Luis Lopez.

What experiences do you think formed your idea of style in those early days?

I remember my first bullfight. You could buy tickets on the sunny side or the shady side of the arena—the sunny side was cheaper, of course. It was a huge spectacle: three bullfighters, nine bulls. At the opening ceremony, the *passeo*, the bullfighter comes out with his ceremonial embroidered cape, the *capote*, which he wears just for show when he first arrives. He walks round the ring, dramatically flourishes the cape in the air, and throws it on the ground in front of the most important person in the audience.

LEFT: Sixties jet set elegance in a printed organza dress for the Spring collection, shot in Santo Domingo, 1968.

I watched . . . and suddenly a whisper went around: "Aaah! Ava Gardner's here!" My God! To me, she was the most beautiful woman in the world. She was wearing a white shirt with the sleeves rolled up, and a belted skirt—very much as people dress today. So I sat there, calculating which exit she'd use to leave the bullring, and I left a few minutes early to be there to see her. The press was already waiting, too, so when she came out, she started running away, with her man friend. Suddenly, I was face to face with her. And I drew myself up and said, "I am Oscar de la Renta and I come from the Dominican Republic!" and she laughed and said, "Oh! How sweet!" Much later, after I'd been in Madrid some time, I saw her again, this time at a cocktail party. I knew my way around by then. I could see she was discussing me across the room with a friend. I went over, and she said "Why don't you come to dinner?" I said "Unfortunately, I'm busy tonight"—which I wasn't—"but maybe later?" So she invited me to a very, very fancy nightclub. And I danced with Ava Gardner. I remember the color of her blue-green

Pat Cleveland demonstrating the eighties version of flounce and ruffle, Summer 1980.

eyes, her very matte skin, her chiseled nose and cheekbones—just unbelievably beautiful.

Spanish traditional costume often surfaces in your work even now. Can you account for that?

I will never forget the importance of my first summer vacation. I bought a book of tickets that gave me 3,000 miles on a train and went all around Andalusia in the south, which had always fascinated me. What I saw has strongly colored my esthetics, the way I have looked at clothes, ever since. I was traveling third class with all the peasants who were on their way to the olive harvest, and there was a whole Gypsy family of about thirty or forty people on board. I ended up being invited to a Gypsy wedding, which went on for three days, and being mesmerized by the sight of all the women wearing flamenco dresses in extraordinary colors. In summertime, there was a *feria*, a festival, in every town, with celebrations, cattle markets, dancing, drinking, horse riding—incredible sights. It was during this trip that I met the bullfighter Antonio Ordoñez.

Gypsy soul. Oscar adapts the Spanish influence for an undone contemporary sexiness, perfectly exemplified by Gisele Bundchen in a ruffled taffeta skirt and silk blouse in New York, 2000.

"His idea: pretty clothes to make women feel attractive," says John Fairchild. Here, Oscar at ease with Nati Abascal in the 1970s.

"What I saw in Spain colored the way I have looked at clothes ever since."

LEFT: The emotional repertoire of Oscar de la Renta's cultural inspiration includes the dramatic sobriety of Naomi Campbell's silk taffeta dress.

RIGHT: The lightheartedness shows in Marisa Berenson's fringed shawl and printed gypsy dress for the Fall 1969 collection.

Statuesque. Iman in a banded satin dress from Fall 1988.

How did you begin to be involved with fashion in Madrid?

It happened by accident. I was having a wonderful time. It was a life of late living—you'd meet friends in a tapas bar at nine, dinner would be at eleven, and I wouldn't get home till three or four. I didn't have to go to school every day, and I learned to go less and less. My father started to pressure me to come back to the Dominican Republic and go into his insurance business. He'd been remarried, to a woman I didn't know, and anyway I couldn't see myself going back at the age of twenty-two. So I needed to generate some extra income, and started doing some fashion sketches for newspapers, magazines, and fashion houses—not that I was making great strides in that, but I was pretending to my father that I was. How much I sold, I don't really remember. Two of my sisters, Avelina and Thelma, who were already married, were helping me with money behind my father's back, too. The sketches were just things in the style of what I'd seen in magazines and newspapers, not very accomplished or technically accurate.

That was about the time you had your first American break—a dress on the cover of Life *magazine?*

You have to understand the political moment to see why this happened. After World War II and the Marshall Plan, Spain was gradually emerging into international acceptance under Franco, and John A. Henry Cabot Lodge, a diplomat from one of the oldest families in the United States, was in Spain as U.S. Ambassador. A dress I had designed for a friend, and had had made up by my tailor, caught the eye of his wife, Francesca, who had an Italian background and was very aware of the arts. After I made a dress for Francesca, she asked me if I would design a dress for her daughter Beatrice for her coming-out party at the American Embassy in Madrid. It was a white tulle double-tiered bubble dress. So the symbolic significance of the girl, the dress, and the moment was resonant enough to put it on the front cover of *Life*. So that was my first American cover, in 1956! I was twenty-four.

How did you come to work for Balenciaga?

At some point I met Pablo Olivera, a decorator who was married to a fabulously eccentric lady named Anna de Pombo, who had designed for Paquin in Paris, and who now held a literary salon in Madrid. You would drop in for a drink in the afternoon, and she would be playing castanets to the sound of Bach. Anna and Pablo were friends of Balenciaga, and she introduced me to him. He asked me to come in and

PREVIOUS PAGE: Nicole Kidman wearing a taffeta bustled skirt and velvet bustier in a *Vogue* shoot about her film *Moulin Rouge*, Fall 2001.

THIS PAGE: "Moving into a new era...with a dazzling heroine." The dynamism of the 1980s, captured in a *WWD* review of Oscar de la Renta, is graphically illustrated by Antonio in one of his ads of the time.

show him my sketches. Balenciaga's business was called "Eisa," because his first house, in San Sebastian, had gone bankrupt, and he was forbidden by law to trade under his name again—which just goes to prove the saying "No one is a prophet in his own land." Because by then, in fashion, Balenciaga was God.

What was the atmosphere like in Balenciaga's house? What work did you do?

My job was to sketch dresses to send to customers with a fabric sample, or several samples in different colors, attached to the drawing—hundreds and hundreds of sketches to send to ladies in the provinces. Today, we send videos or photographed look-books to customers; then it was all sketches. Balenciaga's establishment, Eisa, was the grandest of all in Spain. It was two floors up in the Grand Via, in a place originally built as an apartment. I only saw Balenciaga when he would come from Paris to fit the collection. I would just peek in, terrified. By this time he had such a huge name that he was practically unapproachable. I worked for him in '57 or '58, at the peak of his career. Balenciaga always remained very, very Spanish. For him, his Spanish clientele was very important. They would send all the paper patterns from Paris. It was a thriving house, because in fact even some of his American clientele would go to him in Madrid, because Spain was becoming a tourist attraction in the 1950s, and it was so much less expensive than Paris.

What did you learn from Balenciaga?

I'd never been to fashion school, I was an art student, so thus far my sketches were all illustrations, not working drawings. So all of a sudden I had this amazing advantage. I could go into the sample rooms, look at clothes, see how they were cut and made, touch the fabric and learn about it. Then I could understand properly where to place the dart and the flounce, and from the hand of a master. Balenciaga worked like an architect, constructing clothes like a one-seam coat; he was really cutting new forms. What he said to women was, "You don't have to have the body; I will create one for you." A Balenciaga coat was very famous for the collars being very thrown back, so that if a woman already had a little middle-aged hump, it would give her a straight line. I remember the Marquesa Llanzol, who was the most visible exponent of Balenciaga's elegance in Spain at that moment. She was extraordinary looking, with a long, long neck and her hair in a chignon, with a beautiful little pillbox hat worn way back. I remember her looking incredibly tall and straight.

But after a couple of years, you became restless?

The point came when I decided that if this was something I was going to do seriously, then I'd have to go to Paris. I thought about it for days and days, and finally took all my courage to go to Mr. Balenciaga and I asked him if he would transfer me to the Paris house. He was kind, but said, "No, you should stay here a year longer to learn your craft." Probably he was totally right. But I wasn't that patient.

Carolyn Murphy, exquisitely dangerous in a silk chiffon waterfall halter and a punched silk faille skirt, Fall 2001.

How did you realize your ambition of going to Paris?

In 1959, I took a vacation and caught the train to Paris. Believing that you should start at the top, and then scale your way down, I went to Christian Dior. This was at a time when Yves Saint Laurent had just left, and they were hiring someone new, Marc Bohan, but his appointment was still a heavily guarded secret. Madame Marguerite, head of the studio, received me and saw my sketches, which by then had become very good. So they hired me on a very minimal salary, starting in two weeks. She told me the studio was being reorganized. I was so excited. But the world is so small. Walking on air, out onto the Avenue Montaigne, I ran into Jorge Granados, a painter friend from Madrid who was now living in Paris. All excited, I told him I was trying to be a fashion designer and had just been hired by Dior. He said, "Well, I'm a very good friend of Antonio Castillo at Lanvin, and I know he's looking for an assistant. Would you like to see him?" I agreed, he called up from the phone booth on the street, and half an hour later I was at Lanvin, in Castillo's studio on the Faubourg Saint-Honoré.

Why were you tempted by the proposition of working for Antonio Castillo instead of Dior?

The point was that the position was to be Castillo's assistant, better than any job I'd have had at Dior. Also, in truth, I spoke very little French, and Antonio Castillo was totally Spanish. He'd started in Paris with Fulco di Verdura, at Chanel in the 1930s, making jewelry, then he'd been to the United States and designed couture for Elizabeth Arden, and then Marie-Blanche de Polignac, Madame Lanvin's daughter, had hired him. So the label in the clothes was Lanvin–Castillo. He asked me a lot of questions. Did I know how to drape, cut? I'd never in my life done any of it, but exaggerated my experience at Balenciaga so I practically became his most important assistant. He offered me a job on the spot, but when I told him I'd already been hired at Dior, he offered me a little more.

But you knew you weren't really qualified for the extremely skilled job you'd just taken. How did you get around that?

I bought time by saying I had to go back to Spain and collect my things. Then I went straight out and looked up the biggest advert for a fashion school in the Yellow Pages. Then I called up the lady and asked if she could teach me everything she knew in the space of two weeks.

Soft, sexy seventies. Printed halter dress shot in Spain from Summer 1971.

Oscar de la Renta arrived in Paris in the early 1960s—action-packed years that thrust fashion to the brink of a revolution. Yves Saint Laurent had just been expelled from Christian Dior after a Left Bank-inspired collection that included a black crocodile motorcycle jacket and mink crash helmet. In the movies, the crop-haired gamine Jean Seberg was a sensation in Jean-Luc Godard's *Breathless* and, in the nightclubs, Paris teenagers were dancing the twist. In 1961, the year of Oscar's appointment at Lanvin-Castillo, André Courrèges (a former assistant of Balenciaga) set up his own couture house and Hubert de Givenchy (another close admirer of the Spanish master) designed Audrey Hepburn's costumes for *Breakfast at Tiffany's*. Although the world was beginning to feel the first seismic rumbles of the youth movement, the grand dictatorship of the old-world system of haute couture was still unchallenged.

his was the milieu of Antonio Castillo, a Spaniard who, after learning his couture skills in Paris, had gone to New York to design for Elizabeth Arden and then returned to work at Lanvin under the Lanvin-Castillo label. His wasn't an avant-garde Left Bank approach; the house was an oasis of extravagantly pretty clothes firmly in line with the desires of grown-up society. Oscar de la Renta, with his charm, good looks, and innate decorative flair, was a quicklearner, picking up skills from Castillo's hands and learning how to operate under the strict rules of the system—and how to bend them just enough to have a little fun. Almost every night, Oscar would end up at Régine's, the definitive Parisian discotheque where Catherine Deneuve and Roger Vadim, Elizabeth Taylor and Richard Burton would dance among the young and beautiful of Paris—a crowd hand picked by the eagle-eyed Régine herself. (She quickly had Oscar down as such a great exponent of the twist that he rarely had to buy his own drinks.) Everything de la Renta learned in those two intense years was to contribute crucially to the kind of designer he was to become in his own right: a man skilled in the arts of exquisite flattery in clothing. By the end of this period, however, he was becoming restless. To this young, ambitious man, it was becoming obvious that the future of fashion lay not in haute couture, but in ready-to-wear. However, Paris, in its myopic way, was slow in catching up with this new reality. Oscar de la Renta began to realize his next dream: moving to America.

What do you remember of your debut at Lanvin-Castillo?

The grand atelier was run by a lady called Madame Yvonne, a very imposing lady. Castillo had selected one of my sketches to be made into a toile, a soft dress with a big bow at the side. During the fitting, I saw her struggling with the bow and not quite managing to tie it, so I stepped in and tied it just so. Monsieur Castillo said "Ah, that is the perfect bow!" and as the words came out of his mouth I felt a sharp pain in my arm. Madame Yvonne had stabbed me with a pin, exclaiming, "Oh, pardon, Monsieur!" I learned my lesson very quickly—you could say something, but never interfere in a fitting.

What were the clothes like at Lanvin-Castillo?

My work through all that period was very Balenciaga-influenced, and so, probably, was everybody else's. But Castillo, like Balenciaga, had a very Spanish influence, especially in his evening clothes . . . a lot of Goyaesque things, lace, pink satin—always the essence of femininity, very elegant.

How did a Paris couture house operate in the early 1960s?

Things were very different then. There were so many great fabric houses, most of which have gone now. Each one would come and present fabrics on consignment. So there was a fabric room next to the studio, and if you wanted to make a suit in pink crepe, you'd have fifty fabrics in five different shades. Bolts and bolts and bolts of fabric, and feathers and jewelry, and trimmings. We would select the fabrics, Castillo would go away, and the other assistant, Dominic Toubeix, and I would sketch. I'd always hate Dominic, because he had three hundred sketches and I'd have forty! Then these sketches would be on Castillo's desk when he came back. He'd do sketches of his own, and maybe pick something of yours, and change it—that's how the collection happened.

Did you get to see the clients?

Castillo was very nice to me—he used to give a lot of dinners, and whenever he needed an extra man, he'd invite me. I'll never forget the first time I saw Gloria Guinness. I'd eavesdrop on Castillo's conversations and heard him saying she was going to lunch with him at Maxim's, just around the corner from Lanvin on the Faubourg Saint-Honoré. So that day, I left for my lunch hour five minutes early and hid in a corner on the street to see her. Everyone on the street turned around to look at her. It was early spring and she was wearing a white Balenciaga suit with a short, loose jacket, with the three-quarter length sleeves he did, white gloves and tiny-heeled, long, low Roger Vivier heels. Her very dark hair was up in a French twist. She had a long, long neck and a pillbox perched way back on the back of her head. Just impeccable. Gloria loved Castillo's evening dresses. Years later, when I had just started to work for myself, my wife Françoise and I were staying with Gloria in Palm Beach, because I had a show down there. I asked her what she'd done with her Balenciaga clothes, and she told me she'd donated them to the Victoria & Albert Museum in London, but said, "I still have all my Castillo dresses, because they're timeless." Antonio was a designer who never really specifically marked a period of fashion, but just made beautiful clothes, especially evening wear.

When did you first meet Françoise de Langlade, who was to become your wife?

Françoise was at that time fashion editor at French *Vogue*, and Edmonde Charles-Roux was editor in chief. I would see Françoise at shows, from afar, that's all. I clearly remember I'd designed a dress that was extremely fragile, a blue cocktail dress with a coat with ostrich feathers glued on it, one by one. The dress was called "The Blue Angel." I was all excited when I heard *Vogue* was going to photograph it, and I said "I'm taking it to the studio myself, because I don't want anyone else touching it." *Vogue* used to have a studio right across the Place du Palais Bourbon from the office. The photographer was William Klein—he was working with neon light, waving it in the air, shooting it to superimpose the light patterns. So that was really the first time I spoke to Françoise, while I was patiently waiting for the coat to be photographed.

You were an assistant, and she was a powerful fashion editor. So how did your relationship take off?

We never dated until I went to New York, but I was always aware of her. You had to be: she was an extraordinarily chic, vibrant person. Françoise dressed very, very simply, almost always in sweaters and skirts and low-heeled Roger Vivier shoes and bags from Madame Guerin. Those bags had gold chain straps from Cartier, interchangeable from bag to bag. She wore Balenciaga or Chanel, mostly sweaters and skirt suits, because she was a working editor and it was the easiest. She decided to do that because every time she went to lunch with Coco Chanel, which happened every Wednesday, she'd get into trouble. Chanel was a nut about the fit of a sleeve, obsessed with it being set in high and tight, so that you could lift your arm. Françoise knew that if she'd turn up in a Chanel jacket, she'd get the lady in the atelier into trouble because Mademoiselle would find something wrong with the fit. Françoise told me that she turned up at Chanel once wearing a new Balenciaga suit, thinking she looked absolutely great. Chanel and Balenciaga were friendly, but rivals, too. So Coco looked at Françoise and said, "Fix your hair!" and when she lifted her arm, the whole suit rode up. Coco looked at her and said, "Funny, I thought he was a good designer!"

At what point did you begin to outgrow your position at Lanvin?

Castillo was never very strong in tailoring, much stronger in evening clothes. Just before I left, I designed a tweed coat, fitted in the front, with pleats, and rounded and loose in the back, with a very Balenciaga collar, set back. Suddenly *Women's Wear Daily* wanted it for the cover. But Castillo wasn't a very good sketcher, either, so he called me at home and asked me to come to his house to sketch it because *Women's Wear Daily* was coming to pick it up to send it to New York right away. I was so proud I'd designed that coat, though I didn't expect any credit for it. I'll never forget: as I handed him the sketch, he looked me in the eye and said, "I knew that when I designed this coat, it was going to be great." I was stunned, and told Dominic the next day, "You know what, he's forgotten I designed that coat," and he said, "Don't be a fool, he did not forget. He's never going to acknowledge it, even to you. You're working for him—it's his coat." I thought that in private, between the two of us, he might mention something, but that's the way it was then.

So you wanted to move on?

Actually, Castillo was very, very kind to me. I'd always stay in his house in Madrid, and so on. But a few of my friends from other houses, assistant designers like me, were all coming back from New York and talking about how much they were being paid in dollars. So Dominic and I were talking secretly about how maybe we should go to New York. But how would I make the money for the trip? Well, because I had been a painter, I used to design scarves, to a standard 36 x 36 shape, and sell them to scarf houses. There were a lot of them—Leonard, Bianchini, Abraham—they'd bring their scarves on consignment to the houses, and when they were bought, you'd be paid for the design. Dominic would know which ones were mine when they came to Lanvin, so of course, he'd pick mine. It was a whole racket! So that's how I saved the extra money to go to New York. It was eleven years since I had been back home to the Dominican Republic. So I decided to go home, and stop off in New York to see if I could get a job. Secretly, so Castillo wouldn't find out, I had asked everyone I knew with connections in New York for letters of introduction.

RIGHT: "Extraordinarily chic and vibrant." Françoise de Langlade, fashion editor of French *Vogue*, photographed in 1964, was the influential life force who became Oscar's wife in New York in 1967.

FAR RIGHT: Atelier life at Lanvin-Castillo. Oscar joining in the fun of the Feast of Saint. Catherine, the saint's day of couture seamstresses, in the early sixties.

Oscar de la Renta first set foot in New York, the city that was to make his fame and fortune, in 1962. In his luggage was his open sesame: three letters of introduction from Paris that would roll open the gates of fashion and high society to him. One, written by the Vicomtesse Jacqueline des Ribes, recommended the thirty-one-year-old to American fashion's highest priestess, Diana Vreeland, editor in chief of *Vogue*. The second, kindly written by Edmonde Charles-Roux in her capacity as editor of French *Vogue*, introduced him to someone even further up the Condé Nast hierarchy: the visionary editorial director Alexander Liberman, a man who discovered and encouraged creative talents of every stripe. The third was from James Brady, bureau chief of *Women's Wear Daily*, introducing him to the paper's editor in chief, John Fairchild, the man who was to be responsible for the emerging profile of designers in the United States.

> 66 I first wore Oscar in the late 1960s. I love all his clothes, because of his sense of color—there's something very staggering about the combinations he chooses. And he has an amazing sense of what is appropriate for an occasion, formal and informal. It seems to me he's in a category by himself. 99

Nancy Kissinger

a t that time, the fashion scene was still dominated by Paris. Since World War II, names like Norman Norell, Claire McCardell, Bill Blass, Donald Brooks, Bonnie Cashin, and Jacques Tiffeau had made it to the forefront of American fashionable consciousness, but they were the exceptions in a system that still ran along the age-old Eurocentric lines. Twice yearly, department stores and Seventh Avenue manufacturers would head for Paris to buy patterns from the haute couture houses. They would then come back and copy them, line for line. In 1960, the icons of American high society were women like Gloria Vanderbilt, Jackie Kennedy, C.Z. Guest, Babe Paley—the heiresses and wives of millionaires and the great patrons of Paris haute couture. These women tended to dress with more simplicity, but also more attention to immaculate grooming, than their European counterparts. This, after all, was still a world in which a "lady" wore gloves, even to work—if she worked at all. As for the Beat generation and the youthquake to come, those far-off tremors barely registered yet in the ground those uptown ladies walked on.

Fresh from Paris, Oscar de la Renta had therefore arrived with a set of qualifications that would have impressed anyone who knew about fashion. Having worked for Balenciaga and at Lanvin-Castillo, one of the most successful couture houses in Paris, his European experience gave him a huge advantage. Add to that a dazzling smile, impeccable dress, upright presence, self-confidence, and smooth negotiating skills, and the thirty-one-year-old was primed to step onto the American scene with aplomb. Oscar had what it took: a talent for the timeless, refined, feminine design that American women could identify with, plus the personal x-factor of a flair for fantasy that they would fall for in a big way. As with his entrance into Paris, offers were showered on him, left and right.

Oscar de la Renta's talent for sculpting daywear in weightless wool is a lifelong signature. A double-faced wool and cashmere dress and cape from Oscar's first collection at Arden for the Winter collection, 1968.

From Day One in New York, astonishing good fortune paved his way. The first night he arrived in the city, Elizabeth Arden, a woman who would never take "no" for an answer, bombarded Oscar with blandishments to work for her. Even by his standards of fast operating, that was quick work—but it turned out to be nothing compared with the miraculous speed of his social acceptance among the chic and the powerful of New York. Straightaway, he was taken under the wing of C.Z. Guest, who was lauded by many as the best-dressed woman in America, and immediately began to mix in a world populated by politicians and royalty, as well as every social mover and shaker who mattered. Meanwhile, the fashion press was also welcoming. Immediately on his arrival at Arden, on February 25, 1963, *WWD* profiled the "Slim, suave, stripe-suited Parisimportation," who was attracting attention with "a gray flannel coat that looks like something a bullfighter would wear." Oscar de la Renta, it reported, was living in a Park Avenue apartment with two beds, and just about no other furniture. "But," he beamed, "all will fall happily into place with time!"

Just two years after arriving in the city, having worked his way up the Seventh Avenue fashion system, Oscar de la Renta became a name in his own right, with his own collection. The fact that he enjoyed such a pleasurable social life detracted not one iota from the work involved in distinguishing himself as a talent, but it was also Oscar's gift to make the grueling reality of design—choosing fabric, fitting, selling to stores, and promotion—look effortless. From the beginning, however, Oscar clearly understood his market: he would aim to dress the very women with whom he mixed so easily. Like a subtly fashioned couture dress molded from a single piece of material, Oscar de la Renta's life and work merged seamlessly—an art he has excelled at ever since.

In 1967, another blessing came to the young man from Santo Domingo. Françoise de Langlade, editor in chief of French *Vogue*, agreed to marry him. After a romantic transatlantic courtship, Françoise gave up her powerful job and came to set up home with Oscar in New York. Françoise, twelve years Oscar's senior, was a live wire—talented, vivacious, clever, and possessed of immaculate French taste. She was also stunningly well connected: the friends who organized a party in Paris to celebrate her engagement and wish her "bon voyage" included the Duke and Duchess of Windsor, the French Prime Minister Georges Pompidou and his wife, Claude, and Marie-Hélène de Rothschild, the queen bee of French society.

Immediately, Oscar's bachelor apartment, two floors of a brownstone on East 80th Street, became a small hub of New York society. The couple would entertain two or three

Wool suit for the Spring collection for Elizabeth Arden in 1966.

THIS PAGE: Princess Elizabeth of Toro wearing a dress for the Fall 1969 collection in Oscar's showroom during her short career as a model.

OPPOSITE: Model in silk crepe dress for Elizabeth Arden.

Dramatic dress for evening of red Kalifa silk crepe. The
classically simple gown has soft draping and bow detail at the
back.

Designed for Elizabeth Arden by Oscar de la Renta.

Style: 59/607
Price:

times a week. On those evenings, the beautiful, the smart, and the talented would cram around their eight-seated table and discuss the matters of the moment long into the night. Full of energy and creativity, Françoise started her own small decorating business and then went to work for *House & Garden*. The couple's taste for entertaining and decorating began to set New York alight. When Françoise discovered an inexpensive French white wine, La Doucette, and began serving it instead of the then-standard cocktails, she revolutionized fashionable drinking habits—*La Doucette* became the *dernier cri* and shot up in price. That home, where they lived from 1967 to 1970, was opulent and warm. Decorated with blue-and-white patterns inspired by Portuguese tiles, it was exotically European. After that, they moved into a brownstone house once owned by Tallulah Bankhead on East 62nd Street, and in 1977 to an apartment on East 70th Street overlooking the Frick Museum. And with every move, their endless changes and lavish innovations in style were adoringly documented by the interiors magazines and social columns. By the dawn of the 1980s, the de la Rentas had created such

"The man has credentials," says C.Z. Guest, a loyal client since the sixties, here photographed accompanying her friend the Duchess of Windsor to Oscar's showroom on Seventh Avenue.

a force field of glamour and success around themselves that, in December 1980, Carrie Donovan of the *New York Times Magazine* splashed their photograph on a cover story. The headline bowdlerized the title of a book by Calvin Tomkins, *Living Well Is the Best Revenge*, in which the writer had documented the fevered, sparkling scene ignited by the American couple Sara and Gerald Murphy on the French Riviera in the 1920s. Under the title *Living Well Is Still the Best Revenge,* the journalist Francesca Stanfill placed Françoise and Oscar de la Renta front and center in the public imagination as latter-day Gatsby-esque alchemists of the gilded uptown social whirl. For their dinners, Françoise, understanding the dynamic nature of New York society, would invite guests from every sphere, from politics to ballet, the conversation touching on everything except hemlines. The article quoted Françoise's friend art historian John

One of Oscar's early runway shows in New York.

Oscar de la Renta with Jane Derby at Oscar's first show for Jane Derby in the Fall of 1965.

66 Oscar de la Renta, slim, suave, stripe suited. . . a Paris importation heading for the Elizabeth Arden custom department. . .Bullish on color, he thinks in terms of Spanish posters—bold blue and strong yellow. 99

WWD, February 25, 1963

Richardson, declaring, "Françoise is like a controller at Kennedy Airport. She knows who's going up, who's going down, and who's going to make it." Truman Capote, Nancy and Henry Kissinger, Barbara Walters, Alan Greenspan, Norman Mailer, Kim d'Estainville, Gore Vidal, and many talented artists passing through frequented the Napoleonic opulence of those rooms, reclining on red velvet sofas amid a riot of pattern on pattern, under Oscar's Orientalist works of art and the soft light thrown by green lamps. The scene, a fusion of Oscar's taste for the romantic and Françoise's Gallic know-how, was New York's closest equivalent to a latter-day Parisian cultural salon. Alexander Liberman compared the flocked red velvet walls edged in faux marble, silk-upholstered Second Empire chairs, mother-of-pearl cabinets, and windows swagged in heavy fringed silk to a stage set. And when the actors entered, they were in costume: Françoise and Oscar's impeccable standards of elegance meant people made a big effort to dress for the occasion. John Richardson noted, "Jeweled women in jewel-colored dresses...French ladies in tulle and diamonds recalling Winterhalter."

Meanwhile, the de la Rentas' weekdays were a perpetual round of charity events, fashion shows, openings, operas, plays, concerts, balls, lunches, and dinners at La Grenouille, La Côte Basque, and La Caravelle—all in the company of women who would make their exits and their entrances swathed in the unmistakable color, flounce, and dash of Oscar de la Renta's luxurious gowns. Although never officially involved in the company, behind the scenes Françoise would drum up enthusiasm, call friends up to come to the shows, and tirelessly add zing to the proceedings.

But there was another, equally important dimension to the lives of Oscar and Françoise. In spite of seeing themselves constantly in the gossip columns, a sense of home and privacy was essential to their well-being. Françoise had been a close friend of Alexander Liberman and his wife, Tatiana, even before Oscar came to New York; now the couple spent weekends with them in their small country house, which they'd bought for a song in Connecticut in the early 1960s. The Libermans' exuberance and intellectual curiosity, combined with their informal style of country living, epitomized how the de la Rentas wanted to be, and where they wanted to live. They fell in love with the wide-open landscapes of Connecticut near the Libermans, and saved all they could to buy a tumbledown clapboard house and disused stables, a property that never-theless commanded magnificent views of rolling hills and forests.

That house in Kent was to become Oscar de la Renta's home, and a life's project for him. It is there that he became drawn to gardening, an obsession he subsequently gave expression to on an ever grander scale in the Dominican Republic and England. Crucially, too, the opportunity to escape from New York City on weekends, from the noise and pressure, allowed Françoise and Oscar emotional balance. In spite of their outward social success, they made a strict pact about keeping time for themselves alone. It was in those years, with Françoise, that Oscar first achieved the harmony in which he has always believed. His definition of living well is that the time you devote to the

Lauren Hutton wearing a silk crepe top and shorts made of beaded silk organza flowers for the Spring collection, 1967.

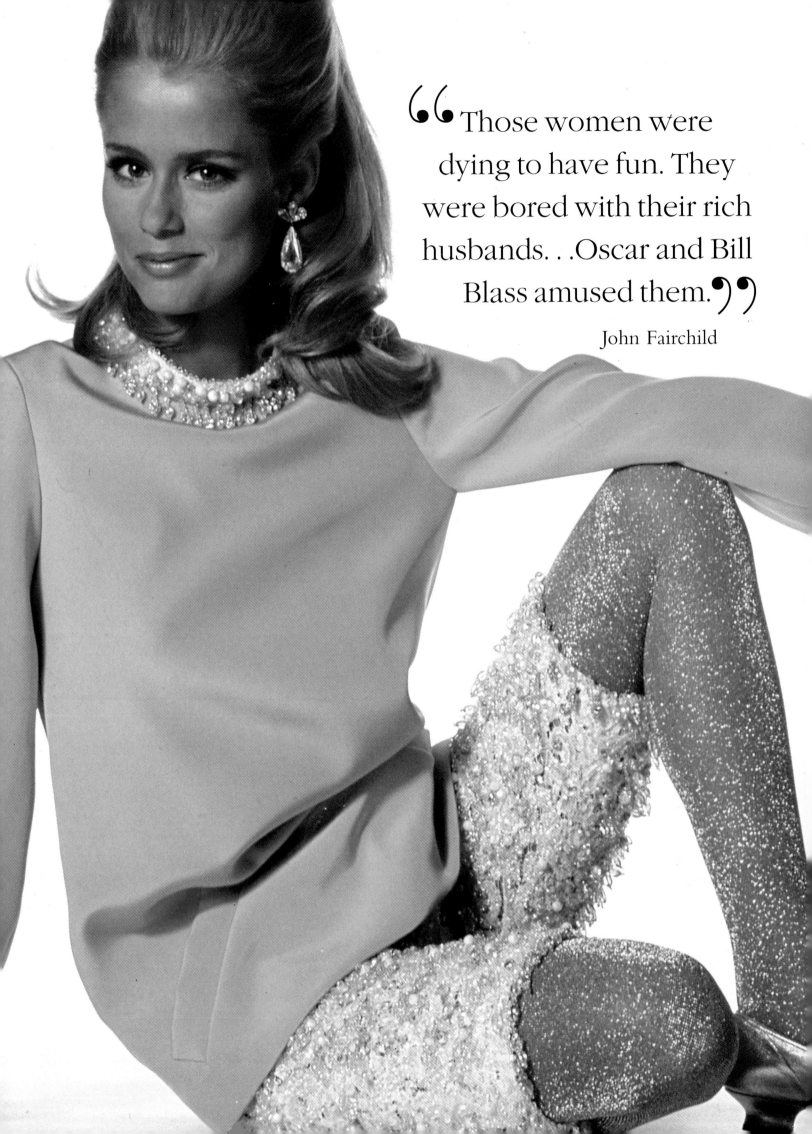

"Those women were dying to have fun. They were bored with their rich husbands. . .Oscar and Bill Blass amused them."

John Fairchild

people you love is as valid a measure of success as anything you achieve at work. It was the memory of those dynamic years of living the good life with Françoise that gave him strength later, when she contracted breast cancer. After a long battle, fought in absolute privacy and resolute optimism to the last, Françoise died in 1983. Now one of the most successful designers in America, twenty years after arriving in New York, Oscar was forced to face his worst fear again: having to live alone.

Take us back to 1963. How did your New York adventure begin?

I'd written to a man named Count Lanfranco Rasponi, telling him I was arriving to stay at the Winslow Hotel on Madison and 55th. The afternoon I arrived, he called me on the telephone and asked, "Do you have a tuxedo?" Fortunately, I did. Lanfranco was in public relations and was helping a fundraiser for the Spoleto Festival that night at the Plaza Hotel. He had taken a table, invited me, and asked if I'd come and pick up the wife of Joshua Logan, the film director, because her husband wasn't in town. So I went as an extra man. Lanfranco did public relations for Elizabeth Arden, and he put me next to her because he knew that I was looking for a job, and that she had a vacancy for a designer for her custom-made collection.

How did you come to work at Elizabeth Arden?

I knew that Antonio Castillo had worked there; he'd told me a lot about her. In fact, she'd sponsored a lot of young talent—Charlie James and Count Sarmi had worked there, as well as Castillo, who had been there five years. When we got into conversation at the table, I pretended I knew very little about it, but I knew very well that she couldn't stand the fact that Castillo had left her. So, suddenly, she recognized in me the great opportunity to get even with him—to steal one of his assistants. Miss Arden quizzed me the whole evening about whether I'd like to come to work in New York. I didn't want to let her know that was my plan, so replied, "Well, eventually maybe yes—but right now I'm

very happy in Paris. But maybe in the future I'd come if I had an offer I couldn't refuse." At the end of the evening, Miss Arden asked me if I would come and see her, and bring my sketches. I said, "Oh, I'm very flattered, but I'm not prepared—I don't have a portfolio with me." Then I suddenly remembered I had a few little sketches I was taking to show my sisters in Santo Domingo, but I'd be too embarrassed to show them to her. Of course, I'd been working on them a whole month! Finally, not sure if she really meant it, I wrote my number on my place card and left. Next morning at ten o'clock, she asked me to go up to see her at Arden. She riffled through my sketches very quickly, and asked me on the spot, "Do you want to work for me?" I repeated I wasn't looking for a job. "But if you had an offer you couldn't refuse?" she insisted. So I took all my strength and said, "Well, I would never work for less than $700 a week," and she shot back, "You have a job!" She was offering a fortune. In Paris, I was being paid something like $500 a month. I was very excited, but said, "Miss Arden, this is quite a surprise. I need to think about it. I have to get advice."

So you went to Diana Vreeland for career advice?

I called Diana Vreeland, and she asked me to have tea with her on a Sunday. By that time, I had a dilemma. I'd met Mary McFadden, who was doing public relations for Christian Dior—they were making a ready-to-wear collection for America. Their designer had left and gone back to Paris. I went up to the Vreelands' red apartment at 550 Park Avenue. She was wearing a caftan, and so was Reed, her incredibly elegant husband, who came into the room for a minute. By this time I had two job offers. Diana asked in a dramatic manner, "Well, young man, what is it that you want to do?" I explained that I'd come to New York because I believed the future of fashion was in ready-to-wear. I was convinced that she'd tell me to go to Dior. But to my surprise, she declared, "In that case, you should go to Elizabeth Arden!" My English wasn't fantastic at that time, and I thought she'd misunderstood what I was saying, because Arden only did custom-made. But she rapped the table. "I understood you perfectly well! Elizabeth Arden is not a designer, but she has launched the career of many designers. At Christian Dior, you will be working under a very powerful name, whereas everyone knows Elizabeth Arden is not a designer, she's a beauty queen. She spends a tremendous amount on advertisements, so you're going to get very good press, and you'll be able to make your name much faster." So I turned down the job at Dior, and for the next two and a half years, I worked at Arden. The label read "Oscar de la Renta for Elizabeth Arden."

You were thirty-one, a stranger in New York. How did you get settled in?

The first person I called when I came to New York was my Spanish friend Count Domingo Vega de la Ren, who had become very close to C.Z. Guest and her husband Winston, after C.Z. had decided she was passionate about learning Spanish. 'Mingo, as we called him, was meant to teach her, though they never got very far with that! C.Z. became very important in my early life in New York. She was the very best-dressed American woman at that point, and wore strictly and only Mainbocher. She had a grand house called

Married at last. Oscar with Françoise the day after their wedding in their New York apartment.

"Templeton" on Long Island—servants everywhere, French butlers, French cooks, and a great variety of people. Her husband hated to go out, and so 'Mingo would accompany her to all the charity balls Winston wouldn't go to. 'Mingo invited me to lunch at Templeton, and C.Z. liked me and invited me for the weekend. Eventually, I had my clothes and a room at Templeton; I went every weekend and it was my life. I had no family in the country, so C.Z. and Winston became my family. Through them, I met a lot of people—Babe and Bill Paley, Truman Capote, Cecil Beaton, the Duke and Duchess of Windsor. The duchess loved to talk. She wore Mainbocher, too.

Photographs of the Duchess of Windsor don't explain what made her so attractive that a king would abdicate for her sake. What was it about her?

She could talk to you and you would be totally mesmerized by what she was saying. She was like Sheherezade. I danced flamenco, and the duchess liked flamenco. She adored Françoise—who they knew in Paris—and nicknamed her "My Vitamin A," because she brought so much enthusiasm and pep to life. They loved Spain and were thinking of buying a home there, and the duke liked to try out his Spanish with me. I remember how he was so particular that people should address the duchess by her correct title. Americans, being so friendly, could be clumsy about addressing royalty. One time the duke was staying at Templeton for the weekend, and I drove him to play golf at a nearby course. I watched. He was a very good player, and as the game progressed people were feeling at ease. He made a shot and a man called out, "Edward, that was wonderful!" The Duke looked at him and said, "You know, it's funny, most people call me Your Majesty or sir. My mother used to call me David, but no one has ever called me Edward."

What are your strongest memories of nights in New York?

Truman Capote was one of C.Z.'s greatest friends, and Truman loved Françoise. That's why I was the only fashion designer to be invited to the ball Truman gave for Katherine Graham at the Plaza in 1967. All the famous ladies came—Babe Paley, Gloria Guinness, Marella Agnelli, Christiana Brandolini—it became a symbol of the period. Black and white had to be worn, so Françoise and I went as a black cat and a white cat. What I remember is having a row with Cecil Beaton. Françoise and I weren't married yet. He couldn't stand her, as at that time French *Vogue* wasn't using him as a photographer. I overheard Cecil ask C.Z., "How can such an attractive young man be having an affair with that ghastly woman?" I'm Latino. I went straight back at him.

Françoise was still editor in chief of Vogue *in Paris. How did you manage your relationship?*

She would come to New York, or I'd go to Paris because my contract from Arden provided that I could spend a month there each year to research. We began dating in 1964. The following year, I left Arden to start my own business. I got my first Coty Award in 1967, for a collection called "The Road of Spices," and I was working hard, and that was the crunch. I said either you marry me or we cool it. So, very gutsily, she gave up her job

"What fascinates me is folklore, how people dress in different cultures." Oscar's research into the roots of folk costume is the source of the rich pattern and vibrant color expressed in his collections from the beginning. Here, a tapestry-influenced coat in velvet, shot on a Basque beach for Fall 1968.

and moved to New York. It was a low-key wedding. We had the marriage license, and needed a witness, so one day I called 'Mingo and invited him to lunch. When I told the taxi driver to take us to City Hall, he said, "Oh my God, I'm not dressed!" Françoise was wearing a little Chloé dress by Karl Lagerfeld. So we sat with all the other couples and waited our turn. It was very romantic in a certain way.

Did Françoise work with you? Did she influence your design?

In fact, we disagreed often on the subject of fashion. I have an affinity for entrance-making clothes. Françoise couldn't identify with that kind of dressing. She had a uniform of sweaters, skirts, pearls, and handbags. She was minimal before minimalism existed. For Françoise to arrive someplace and be noticed for what she was wearing was terrible. She didn't work at Oscar de la Renta, but she was a real pro. She could go and see a collection and tell me how wonderful it was in front of people, and then go home and say, "How could you do something so horrible?" But for everything she did in our lives together in New York, and for our happy times and all the people we met and became our friends, I have Françoise to thank.

How did you survive losing Françoise?

I was totally devastated when Françoise died. She was the most important presence in my life up to that point. We were devoted to one another. When she died in 1983, at four in the morning, Annette Reed, who was a great friend of both of ours, was the first person I called at six o'clock. Annette and Mica Ertegun looked after me constantly at that time and, knowing how I hate to be by myself, made sure I was busy every night. Annette was married at the time and is a very, very private person. There was absolutely no suggestion of any romance at that moment, but after many years, Annette was to be the person who put my future life together again. I fell intensely in love with her, and eventually persuaded her to marry me in 1987. I have been so very lucky in my life. The most important thing that has happened to me is that I have married two very extraordinary women.

OPPOSITE: A passion for dance. A timeless silk organza dress from 1971.

FOLLOWING PAGE RIGHT: Social magnets. Oscar and Françoise on the cover of a *New York Times Magazine* article titled "Living Well Is The Best Revenge," by Francesca Stanfill in 1980.

“His clothes give you such a wonderful feeling.
The first time I put on one of his dresses, I felt like
a fairy. His evening things make you feel like
you’re walking on air.”
Brooke de Ocampo

Oscar de la Ginza

WWD

THURSDAY, OCTOBER 6, 1977
VOL. 135 NO. 68 • 35 CENTS

U.S. interest spurs British spring hope

See INCREASES, page 11

TODAY

Kayser-Roth deal for Gemcos companies falls through — Page 18

West Point-Pepperel closing fabrics plant in Texas — Page 11

Jantzen net drops 53.6 percent for year — Page 10

Hoechst fibers lose $48 million in half

cue

March 12, 1966   25¢

european designers in new york

VOGUE

SEPT.

special 300-page issue

AMERICAN FASHION

80 GREAT NEW LOOKS
and how to wear them

THE NEW YORK COLLECTIONS

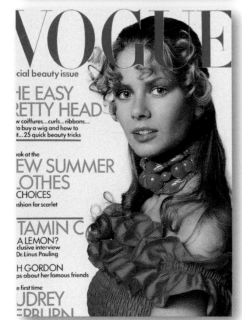

VOGUE

special beauty issue

THE EASY PRETTY HEAD

new coiffures...curls...ribbons...
how to buy a wig and how to
wear it...25 quick beauty tricks

look at the
NEW SUMMER CLOTHES
CHOICES
fashion for scarlet

VITAMIN C
A LEMON?
exclusive interview
Dr. Linus Pauling

RUTH GORDON
raps about her famous friends

the first time
AUDREY
HEPBURN

FEB. 1972   HARPER'S

BAZAAR

IN DEFENSE OF NEW YORK / OUR INTIMATE ACTS
ANTI-SEMITISM '72 / MAVERICK: MARY LINDSAY
N.Y.'S FASHION INFLUENTIALS (BELOW; INSIDE)

"There should always be
some small surprise for guests...
a new way of doing
the flowers . . . or something different
with the food."

Françoise de la Renta is keenly aware of those delights to the senses in which a house must be rich . . .

he New York Times Magazine
MBER 21, 1980/SECTION 6

ING
LL
STILL THE
ST REVENGE
ncesca Stanfill
Franco
Oscar de la

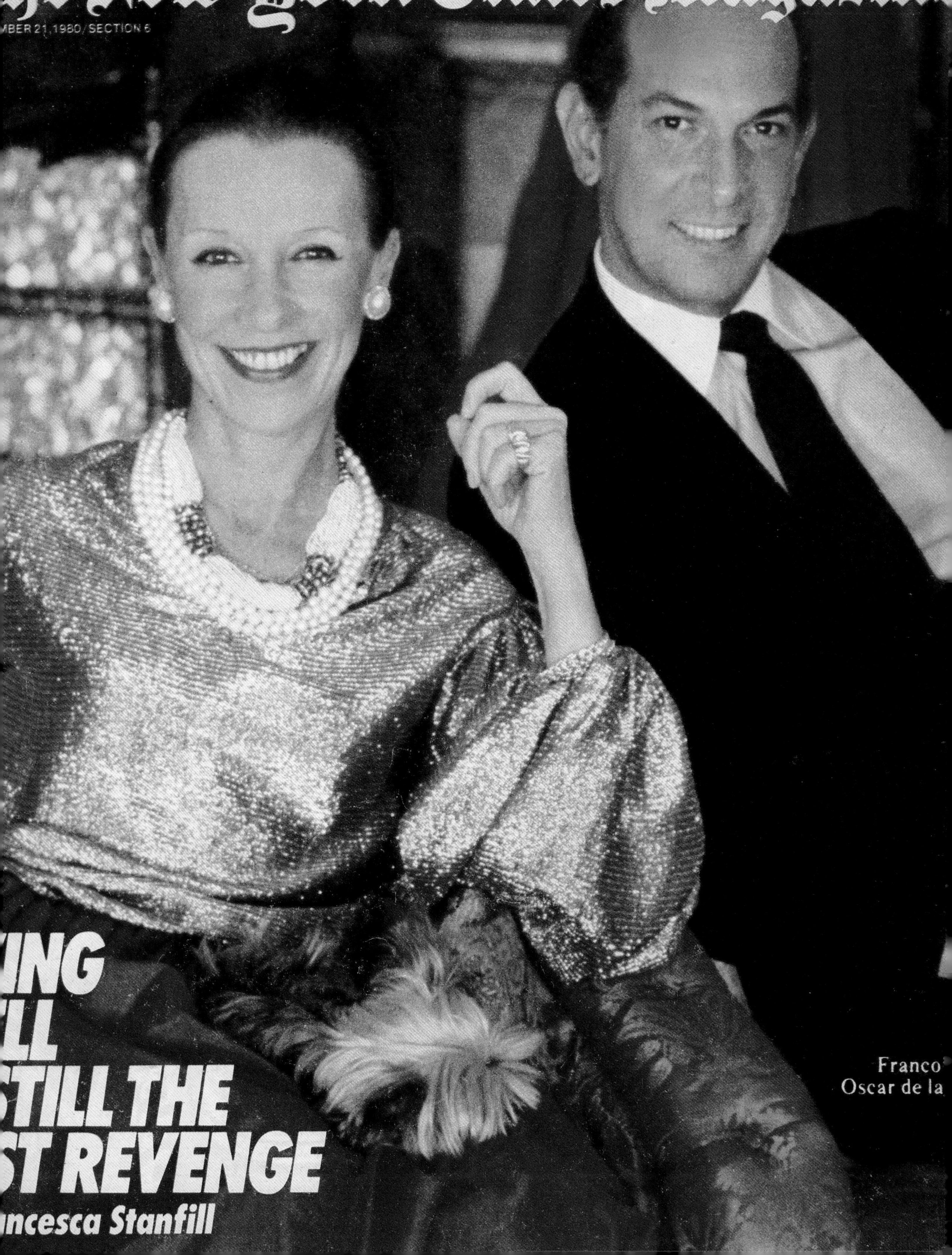

The changing fashion scenes Oscar de la Renta has witnessed over more than forty years are almost beyond imagining. He was there at the zenith of the old-world European haute couture, a keen-eyed observer when ready-to-wear was taking off, and then—ready, willing, and able—destined to become a key participant in the new world order that put American fashion on the map for the first time in history. He was there when the youthquake of the 1960s shook the foundations of the known fashion world. He participated in the jet-set 1970s and shone in the gilt-edged 1980s. More than that, his life and extraordinary times represent an incalculable rise in the status of the successful fashion designer that took his generation way beyond being mere makers of beautiful clothes to the position that now seems almost natural and inevitable—that of contemporary celebrities, players in the big league of American social life.

OPPOSITE: Uptown, par excellence. The dash and verve of the New York sixties and seventies, perfectly exemplified by Oscar's wool cape and tweed pants for Winter 1969.

THIS PAGE: Hooded mink by Oscar de la Renta for Oliver Gintel and stretch boots by David Evins for Oscar de la Renta, 1967.

h ow refreshing, then—and instructive—to find Oscar de la Renta loath to rest on any laurels. His memories of all the steps, all the parties, all the acquaintances and friends—and all the long nights of hard work in his studio—that have taken him to the top are as fresh as yesterday. The tale of his climb to his privileged place in the power circles of New York and Washington high society is one thing, but what's kept him there, and in business, is another. The ability to keep moving with the beat of the times, and to calculate exactly what that means for the changing lives of the class of women he dresses, takes constant watchfulness, relentless work, endless travel. Relevance to the market doesn't stay with people who live in ivory towers—even if they are dealing in the currency of glamour.

When Oscar de la Renta began his career on Seventh Avenue, opportunities for celebrity were, in any case, thin on the ground for designers, even if their customers were names to conjure with. In the early 1960s, manufacturers wielded the power, dressing the masses in knockoff Paris lookalikes to be sold across the nation in department stores. Oscar de la Renta's first stop, at Elizabeth Arden, had given him one important advantage in the climb to public recognition: the label in her custom-made collection read "Oscar de la Renta for Elizabeth Arden," just as Diana Vreeland had anticipated. After a year and a half, though, he was restless. Arden's clothes were custom-made, and Oscar spent months cajoling his boss to move to where the action was: ready-to-wear.

Miss Arden, listening to Oscar's energetic ideas, agreed to send her young designer to talk to a Seventh Avenue manufacturer, Benjamin Shaw, who was already backing Geoffrey Beene, Donald Brooks, and Jane Derby. At the last minute, Arden changed her mind, but Oscar's next move was sealed: it was he who went into business with Benjamin Shaw, not Arden. Shaw appreciated the potential of Oscar's talent. He needed a designer to work for Jane Derby, and again the formula gave Oscar's name prominence. When Jane Derby died six months later, his name alone appeared on the label. Oscar de la Renta was finally in business in his own right. It was 1965.

Fashion, by now, was turning wild, unpredictable, and young. Miniskirts, op art, and Beatlemania were all in the air. Rudi Gernreich came up with a topless swimsuit and a "no-bra bra" and, in Paris, André Courrèges had taken a giant leap into the future with his space age collection. But Oscar de la Renta was no revolutionary, and neither were the ladies he knew he wanted to dress. Instead, he set out on a mission to translate the youth vibe, making it appropriate for the uptown tribes of women who existed in every major city across America.

What did that mean? De la Renta's hemlines could inch above the knee at exactly the rate at which mothers wanted to keep up with their daughters—and at precisely the length currently acceptable at twenty-one inches. Then, when the counterculture of Haight-Ashbury and Woodstock made national news, Oscar found a way to turn his customers—hardly the dropout type—on to the psychedelic experience. His was the New York version of the hippie fashion trip, strictly for first-class travelers, of course.

TOP LEFT: A seamless connection between life and work. Oscar fixing a bridesmaid's dress in the 1970's.

TOP RIGHT: Oscar with models on the runway for his Spring 1993 collection in Paris.

MIDDLE LEFT: People watching a video featuring Oscar.

MIDDLE RIGHT: Oscar de La Renta speaking with Luigi, his tailor in Paris in 1993.

BOTTOM LEFT: Oscar and Françoise arriving in Houston to accept the Neiman Marcus Award in 1967.

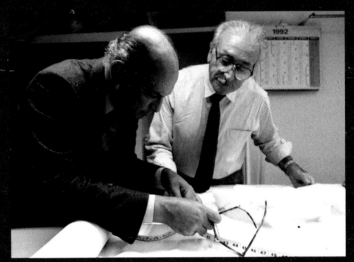

VOGUE

FEBRUARY

100
SPRING
LOOKS

FROM SIMPLE TO
SENSATIONAL

THE MAN
BEHIND
ANNE KLEIN
WHATEVER

Bravado...reve

Oscar de la Renta loves   all the girls...

¡HOLA!
NUMERO EXTRAORDINARIO

550 PESETAS

ALTA
COSTURA
OTOÑO-
INVIERNO
1999-2000

Esther Cañadas, con traje
en ante beige, destacado collar y espectacular chal en
visón tricotado de Balmain.

TOWN & COUNTRY
ESTABLISHED IN 1846

A Splendid
Spring

Couture Blooms Again

An Enchanting Inn
in Italy

Sapphire's Fresh Colors

Entertaining in the
Napa Valley

1999
CANADA $5.90
FGN $5.90

WWD
READY-TO-WEAR REPORT

Bendel's new unit on 5th loo
to recapture former cachet /

Federated/Allied scores almo
$75M profit in December / 17

Oscar
Plays
A Long
Suit

NEW YORK —
time for the gre
length debate a
"Too short is a
short," says Os
la Renta, who's
with several len
fall — from a fe
inches above th
to midcalf. "A
longer length is
practical and m
appealing. And
longer looks eve
better." Here, f
collection he wi
first in Paris on
19, the long suit
wool tweed. For
on long versus
see pages 8 an

ear CHH
ops Paying
s Vendors

NEW YORK — Carter Hawley
Stores, Inc., reportedly has hal
ayments to vendors because of a
ere cash-flow crunch.
As a result, most factors have
off credit for DHL, according to
ies, and some vendors have all
stopped shipping.
Carole Little, Inc.
ards Little, Inc.,
ny, president of Judy Knapp, said
ctor told him on Monday to stop

ELLE
WWW.ELLE.COM

SPECIAL
REPORT:
WOMEN,
SEX, AND
SPENDING

FASHION
SPLURGE
YOUR
SPRING
ESSENTIALS

THE NEW
POLITICALLY
CORRECT
ANOREXIA

UMA
IN BLOO
THURMAN ON BE
A WIFE, MOTHER
MILLION DOLLAR

BEAUTY
SPECIAL
SEDUCTIVE HAIR, BOLD MAKEUP

The mood of the moment was an absolute gift for a romantic designer with a highly developed sense of the feminine and the exotic. With his European-educated eye for luxury fabrics and his Latin American love of vibrant color, Oscar hit a unique note on a Seventh Avenue that was more attuned to the simplicity of homegrown sportswear. The Oscar de la Renta reputation for making dreamy fantasies—the distinction that has stayed with him ever since—spread throughout America, splashed on the covers of *Vogue* and *Women's Wear Daily*, and selling like crazy in the department stores.

In those early years, Oscar did Park Avenue caftans, loose pajama shirts, fringed ponchos, and evening vests with the words "Peace," "Groovy," and "Dig It" embroidered in rhinestones and beads. Brocade, paisley, shantung, organza ruffles, vibrant flower prints, and gilt-edged detail made everything he touched luxe and lush. Lace, embroidery, and pretty surface patterns became his signature, adorning entrance-making outfits for the grandest of American formal occasions. In contrast with the inaccessible extremes of European fashion, however, these were clothes designed to be put on. Oscar would never do anything just for a show. His love of fantasy never got in the way of his main objective of making clothes to be worn, not for the museum.

America welcomes talent, and Oscar de la Renta was beginning to fly. In 1967, aged thirty-five, he received real recognition from his peer group for the first time when he designed "The Road of Spices," a sumptuously romantic collection. That collection won him his first Coty Award, the highest fashion accolade possible. The panel of judges was made up of America's most influential fashion journalists. Even better, 1967 was also the year Françoise de Langlade finally agreed to take a taxi down to City Hall and marry him. Happy, settled, and on a roll, he won the Coty Award for the second year running in 1968 with his Belle Epoque collection, with its high necks, leg-o'-mutton sleeves, quilted satins, fragile lace, and rich fur trimmings. In 1969, he became a United States citizen with dual nationality. By 1973, Oscar de la Renta had become so successful that he was finally elected to the Coty Hall of Fame.

As the 1960s turned into the 1970s, American fashion was picking up speed and self-confidence. Clothes became softer and sexier, designed for the new long-limbed, energetic, tawny all-American blondes. Oscar went with the flow, producing gorgeous decorative print gowns to flatter women were going out in the evening—but not necessarily to Studio 54. His understanding of exactly those women came from his own nightly field research, and from his trips across the country to charity events—the road every American designer must take in order to keep in touch and sell. Throughout, he focused on the thing he always considered his most important job in fashion: making his customers look and feel terrific. It was during those early days of his marriage to Françoise that his talented wife, with her French flair and eye for interior design, made their new house on East 62nd Street a magnet for talented, sophisticated guests, where musicians, opera singers, and ballet dancers would mix with politicians and the power brokers of business and high society. It was a scene that was to make headlines.

Oscar and his peer group—Bill Blass, Halston, Ann Klein, Geoffrey Beene—were

now on the rise and beginning to make millions. They decided it was about time to tell the world about it. In 1973, an audacious plan was hatched to take the best of American design to Paris, the stronghold of traditional European power in the fashion world. A joint show was to be staged at Versailles involving five Americans and five French couturiers—an exercise in *entente cordiale* that nevertheless also had the potential to turn into an international fashion showdown. French designers had always regarded themselves as innately superior pacesetters, and their American cousins as, at best, followers in their illustrious wake. It was to be a spectacular social occasion in the presence of Princess Grace of Monaco, with a grand candlelit dinner after the show, which would take place, by special permission of President Georges Pompidou, in the Marie-Antoinette Theater. In the buildup, even *The New York Times* got excited, reporting that "Paris is in a tizzy." The plans, however, were a nightmare of politics and infighting. Behind the scenes, Oscar de la Renta used his secret French weapon: Françoise. Being Parisian herself, she proved the perfect diplomatic agent. On the night, Oscar's gowns brought the show to its finale, and—in spite of all the apprehension—*The New York Times* reported triumphantly that "the night belonged to the Americans." That evening has gone down in Seventh Avenue legend as the one that changed the status of American fashion forever.

By now, Oscar de la Renta had become, as John Fairchild called him, "a social lion." He had also begun to make his fortune. In 1977, he launched his first scent, "Oscar," in a bottle stoppered with a romantic glass flower, a perfume that became a best-seller throughout America. At the turn of the 1980s, with Ronald Reagan in power, fashion again swung into confident, decorative, celebratory mode—Oscar's territory par excellence. With his gold lamé, brocade, romantic bouffant skirts in vibrant colors, and huge airy sleeves, his work once again received a rapturous reception. Every collection was

OPPOSITE: "He's a figure of grace. A warm-hearted, happy, cheerful person." So says Nancy Kissinger, speaking for all of Oscar de la Renta's circle of distinguished women friends. Here, Oscar entertains Candice Bergen in his New York apartment for a *Vogue* magazine shoot in the late seventies.

THIS PAGE: Oscar was in his element in the late sixties, translating exotic bohemianism for the uptown tribes, as in this bead-fringed "Belly Dancing" two piece from 1968.

THIS PAGE: The internationalist. Oscar with Issey Miyake and Karl Lagerfeld in front of The Four Seasons restaurant in New York, from an article titled "East Meets West," from *WWD* in April 1984.

OPPOSITE: The caftan trail. Marisa Berenson in Oscar's sophisticated version of the sixties printed caftan, 1966.

66 Oscar is the kindest man. He has been so successful—and given a lot back. He's made a lot of other people happy: that's success. I admire him. 99

C.Z. Guest

What amazes me about Oscar is that he is involved in everything we do every step of the way. He never stops thinking or working...during the hectic days before a show. You'll inevitably find him in the back with the tailors sewing a button or adding a fur trip on a coat...he's always calm, with a smile on his face enjoying every minute of what's he's doing. **"**

Eliza Reed Bolen

Oscar's winning collections. Carrying off Coty Awards two years running, Oscar de la Renta was on a roll in the late sixties. ABOVE: Nati Abascal wears a caftan with a print inspired by Klimt, from the 1968 "Belle Epoque" collection.

splashed on the cover of *WWD*, picked out by Fairchild as striking symbols of the times.

It was during those years that Oscar de la Renta, trusted designer of stately and opulent clothes with a unique sensitivity to the minute calibrations of flattery versus appropriateness, first came to the attention of the White House. Invited as a guest by Gerald and Betty Ford in the 1970s, he went on to dress Nancy Reagan in the 1980s and, with a smoothness that demonstrates the diplomatic neutrality of the designer's professionalism, became a designer of choice for Hillary Clinton in the 1990s and Laura Bush in the twenty-first century.

How did you manage to reach the position of becoming a designer in your own right?

When I was at Elizabeth Arden, I made arrangements to go and speak to Benjamin Shaw, a Seventh Avenue manufacturer, about ready-to-wear on her behalf. I believed totally that this was the future, but Arden was still only in custom-made. Benjamin Shaw already had an interest in Geoffrey Beene, Donald Brooks, and Jane Derby. But Miss Arden was prone to changing her mind, and someone back in the office was whispering to her that it was a bad move. So I went back to Seventh Avenue and told Mr. Shaw that Miss Arden had decided not to go ahead. Benjamin Shaw was a typical Seventh Avenue entrepreneur, but enlightened, because he understood the role designers could play, and he appreciated what I'd been doing for Arden. He said, "Why don't you come with us? We're not interested in Arden, but in you." So I made a deal with them by which I was going to get an interest of 33% of the company, and I was going to be working as "Oscar de la Renta for Jane Derby," but my name was above and bigger than Jane Derby. Then Jane died six months later, and the label became "Oscar de la Renta," in mid-1965.

Forever '68. As desirable now as it was when it was designed, a multicolored dream dress in psychedelic printed organza.

THE AMERICANS IN PARIS CLOCKWISE FROM TOP LEFT: Oscar with Betsy Bloomingdale, at Versailles post-show party, the evening when Seventh Avenue designers wowed the Paris couture establishment with its energy and modernism, 1973; Oscar's finale of fluid crepe de chine gowns, designed for movement; Oscar dancing with model; Oscar, Halston, the illustrator Joe Eula and Bill Blass outside Maxim's; Liza Minnelli belting it out, surrounded by Anne Klein models; The Marie-Antoinette theater at Versailles; Models descending the stairs with Patrick Honoré dressed as King.

What was the status of Seventh Avenue designers then?

This will tell you: I remember at one point, in 1966, five or six of us—me, Bill Blass, Donald Brooks, Geoffrey Beene—were summoned to the office of Mr. Gimbel, the president of Saks Fifth Avenue, to hear him make a big announcement. When our clothes went into the store, the store would take out our labels and put their name in—and the announcement was that our labels were going to be kept in the garments.

Why did the system begin to change?

The early 1960s in New York were strongly marked by John Fairchild, editor of *Women's Wear Daily*, who was very responsible for bringing designers up front. He would go to the manufacturers and say, "Who is the designer back there? That's who I want to talk to!" Before that, all the interviews would be with the manufacturers. John changed everything. Later, he began to introduce profiles of stylish people into the paper, so it became a social documentary and fashion arbiter of the times. In that way, *WWD* went way beyond a trade publication that only industry people read, and became a powerful opinion-former. I cannot overemphasize how much I owe to John Fairchild. There's no question: he was the most important, and sometimes controversial, force in American fashion. From the time I landed in New York, he believed in me. I owe a lot of my career to him.

What were fashion shows like at that time?

We used to show in the showrooms. There were model agencies exclusively for shows and for cover girls. The girls would come with their own shoes, a pair of pumps for day and one for night, and do their own hair and makeup. My first show had six models. I was one of the first designers to ask cover girls to do the shows. I had people like Penelope Tree and Samantha Jones, who were on every cover of *Vogue*.

Your "Road of Spices" collection in 1967 won your first Coty Award. What inspired it?

I'd been reading a Lesley Blanch novel, *Journey into the Mind's Eye*, which was all about a traveler. During that time, and a bit later, it was all about the flower children, hippies, Afghan coats, Thea Porter, who did beautiful caftans, and all those designers in London.

What references were you calling on during this time?

I have always been attracted by the exotic, no question about it. Rather than looking to the past, I would always look at folklore and how people were dressed in different cultures. I would look at Chinese dress and study the way there would be similarities to Spanish dress, though flamenco has nothing to do with Chinese dress. You can trace the same thread from India to eastern Europe. That's what fascinates me. I have always had a romantic tinge.

How did you perceive your role as a fashion designer?

I have always felt very strongly that my role as a designer is to do the very best I can for a woman to make her look her best. Fashion is only fashion once a woman puts it on. A great spectacular show is one thing, but it doesn't mean anything unless it makes a woman go away wanting to wear what she's seen. My strong philosophy has always been to address the consumer. I've never wanted to seduce the press, but the woman.

How easy was it to gain press recognition?

When I first started with interviews, I always thought I'd turn a negative into a positive. With my name, people always thought I was Spanish or Italian. Journalists show up with the idea of what they're going to write already fixed. Say you come from the Dominican Republic—no story! When I was traveling in the U.S. at first—not so much now—people would sometimes ask if the Dominican Republic was in the Philippines! Other times, people would ask me if I was American, and I'd say, "Yes, I'm from the Dominican Republic. I was American before you were!"

So after winning Coty Awards two years running, you were becoming very well known?

You know, fame in New York doesn't mean fame in America. A lot of European designers make that mistake—coming here and making a splash in New York, and thinking that's it. But once you cross the Hudson River, it's another country. It takes much, much more to be known in the United States. We do masses of trunk shows, and if there was a charity event, a luncheon, or a black tie affair, I would go to it.

American fashion was on the up and up. But it took the Versailles show in 1973 to make a big international statement. How did that come about?

Eleanor Lambert, who was the queen bee of American PR, hatched up the idea with Pierre Bergé at Saint Laurent that five French designers should invite five Americans to come and show at Versailles. It was to be a big social occasion. Françoise and I convinced Baroness Marie-Hélène de Rothschild to host the evening, and I think that is why all the grand people of Paris came—not because of the American designers, but because of Marie-Hélène. We sold her on this idea that Dior, Saint Laurent, Givenchy, Cardin, and Ungaro were going to invite me, Bill Blass, Halston, Donald Brooks, and Ann Klein. There was a big deal about Ann Klein because she was a sportswear designer, and Pierre Bergé, who was in command at Saint Laurent, said she was not a couturier! But, we said, none of us does couture, we do ready-to-wear! Then Joe Eula, who worked with Halston, was going to do the set for the American section, which caused enough problems in itself between everybody—but then he went to Paris to measure up the set, and they gave him centimeters instead of inches, so when it arrived nothing fit! So in the end, we all had to have a black backdrop, which turned out to be a godsend, because it looked so put-together and presented. The French did something very elaborate with a themed float for each designer. What was really essential was that

Vanessa Redgrave wearing a leotard under a rhinestone-studded clear vinyl coat by Oscar de la Renta for Jane Derby, 1967.

LEFT: The model Apolonia wearing a huge embroidered tulle dress in the 1980s.

ABOVE: Sketch for a dress.

BELOW: Françoise de la Renta with Yves Saint Laurent.

RIGHT: Iman modeling a gold lamé skirt and top with embroidered jacket for Fall 1984.

" Each and every costume has such beautiful balance. He has, like Dior, Givenchy and Saint Laurent, a total head-to-toe look and this is so vitally important. "

Diana Vreeland, from a memo, May 8, 1970

we had black models who walked to the music. That was the very first time it was done—girls just swinging out to the pace of the music. Kay Thompson, who had played the Diana Vreeland character in *Funny Face* and was an actress and singer, choreographed the show. And Liza Minnelli opened the show, singing "I want to wander down the Champs-Elysées," which Audrey Hepburn sang in *Funny Face*, as girls dressed in trench coats and carrying suitcases arrived on stage. I had the finale. I did a whole series of fluid dresses in chiffon and satin-backed crepe de chine because I realized how they'd flatter the girls in movement. The whole thing was a huge success. It was the only time French designers have collaborated like that with Americans—before or since.

You were by then playing such a respected role—as a designer and as a diplomat—in the fashion world that you became president of the Council of Fashion Designers of America?

I was the president of the CFDA from 1973 to 1976, and then again from 1986 to 1988, and I created the CFDA fashion awards. Up till then, they had been sponsored by Coty, a fragrance company. By that time, many of us were beginning to become involved with fragrances ourselves, and I saw it would be a conflict of interest. I believed our peers should be in control of the fashion awards, just as the peer group in Hollywood is in charge of the Academy Awards.

You made a huge impact with your first scent in 1977. How did you do that?

That scent, which people know as "Oscar," was probably the very first American classic. It's still my most important and biggest-selling fragrance. With fragrance, you have to have a clear understanding of who the consumer is. We started small and traveled all over the country to talk about it. One lesson I learned is that selling dresses is visual, but when you're selling fragrance, it's a little bit of a mystery, and the girl behind the counter has tremendous influence in talking about that mystery. I realized my job was to make that girl my friend. If she likes you, she will go the extra mile to tell the customer and persuade her to believe in your scent.

Do you think having a scent helps to sell clothes?

It certainly helps to create a total image of the woman you are trying to dress. What's wonderful about a fragrance is that you don't need it the way you need to wear clothes. To wear perfume is a luxury; it's about spoiling yourself with some kind of fantasy. What makes a perfume successful is not when a woman buys it the first time, but the third and fourth. Because by then, she is not buying it because she likes the bottle or thinks the packaging is pretty, she's buying it because she identifies with it. It is hers.

From the 1960s into the 1970s, the 1980s into the 1990s, so much has changed in fashion. How have you kept a sense of your identity against the background of shifting trends?

I always say I survived the late seventies! That time was dominated by Yves Saint Laurent, the pants suit and tuxedo, very mannish. As a designer, it wasn't my bag. In the

PREVIOUS PAGES, LEFT: Victorian splendor. The living room of Oscar's New York apartment shot for *House & Garden* magazine in 1985.

RIGHT: Iman backstage at an early eighties fashion show wearing a velvet dress with embroidered details.

LEFT: Sketch by Francisco Ferreira for the Fall 1995 collection.

Pulled-together business dressing for Fall 1987.

eighties, it was back into rich, opulent clothes, which were my thing. I wasn't a good minimalist in the nineties, but at the end of the decade, there was this new thing about the power of femininity, and that has been great for me again.

At what point did you and Françoise start to be invited to the White House?

We were first invited by President and Mrs. Ford. What a story that was! I was so excited. It was the middle of winter, in the seventies. Françoise and I arrived to stay at the Watergate Hotel and when we were dressing, I put my arm in my shirt, and it wouldn't go in! The maid had packed Françoise's tuxedo shirt instead of mine. So I had no shirt—and it was already 7 P.M. I was totally panicked. So I called the only person I could think of, Ethel Kennedy, and she said, "Give me ten minutes." I waited, she didn't call back, so I called the concierge and begged for a waiter's shirt, but they said the waiters didn't wear white shirts—but I might be able to find a shop still open in the hotel. So I put on my tux without a shirt and ran to the other end of the complex, and the shop was open, and there it was: a shirt with white ruffles, with black edges! So I had to buy it. It was my worst nightmare come true! You know, I really admire people who can wear colored shirts, shirts with flowers on them—but I am always afraid that if I do, someone will say, "Sorry, the Latin band goes in the other door!" That is completely my complex. When I got back to the room, Ben Bradlee of the *Washington Post* had sent over a shirt, but Françoise said, "We are so unbelievably late, you can't change!" So the first time I went to the White House, I was wearing this horrible shirt. Nobody seemed to notice.

You began to dress Nancy Kissinger at that time?

Nancy came to see us when she was engaged to be married to Henry, and was starting to do a lot of entertaining—state dinners and luncheons and so on. They have both become our closest friends. Nancy can wear a lot of clothes—she's unbelievably tall and glamorous, and looks good in big clothes.

Then Nancy Reagan became interested in your clothes. How did you work with her?

We met her in California, when Mr. Reagan was governor. Once she came to the White House, we would send her videos and books and she would pick things out. She was small, a model size, knew what looked good on her, and had a true sense of fashion. Especially after the Nixon years, it was a very good, very glamorous period at the White House. Mrs. Reagan would host a lot of dinners, and I was lucky to be invited to many of them.

Karen Graham wearing a chiffon gown for the Spring collection in 1974.

But then again, much later, you also dressed Hillary Clinton. How do you manage to be such a diplomat that you can appeal to both Republicans and Democrats?

It is not an issue. I voted for President Reagan and I voted for President Clinton. I vote for the people I believe in, not parties. Mrs. Reagan and Mrs. Clinton are two very different, but very strong personalities. Mrs. Clinton was never interested in clothes until she came to the White House. That was the first time she had to worry about it. I really was first asked to help personally for the second inauguration, for which I made a lot of day and evening costumes. Until then, she had worn a lot of black, so I got her to wear a lot of softer colors—pastels are good for her. I figured it would work because immediately it would give her a different image on TV; people would think, "What a nice lady!" But she's prudish! She has a beautiful décolleté, marvelous shoulders, but she didn't see it. I had a rough time with her!

LEFT: The Spring 1993 collection as illustrated by Gladys Perint Palmer.

FOLLOWING PAGES: Oscar de la Renta and Mikhail Baryshnikov, from a book written by Baryshnikov and Peter Anastos with photographs by Arthur Elgort, called *The Swan Prince*, 1987.

The Dominican Republic is where Oscar de la Renta goes to remind himself of who he is. At his Caribbean home in Punta Cana, he can pursue everything he loves, from gardening in the sunshine and entertaining to playing with the children in La Casa del Niño, the school for street children in La Romana that he co-founded and has run since 1982. People who visit him in the Dominican Republic—and there has been a constant, dizzying parade of stellar guests at every holiday down the years—get to see Oscar as he really is: a relaxed, urbane, gregarious Latino, a master orchestrator of the arts of living well and making people feel good. But they see something more important, too. The de la Renta house in Punta Cana may be a domain built forpleasure, laughter, and easy living, but the routine there is not one of nonstop lotus-eating.

Oscar's home in Santo Domingo. The house was designed by Cuban-born architect Ernesto Buch. It is built of coral rock quarried on the island, and was inspired by a classic Barbados plantation house.

“ At his house, everything is peaceful and quiet. There’s tennis, walking, swimming, and riding, which my husband loves. It’s relaxed. You do what you want. ”

Nancy Kissinger

66 Oscar loves simple things—a sunset, a sunrise, music above all. He sings, he dances, he whistles—he loves people, has a real appreciation of life. When he comes into a room, he brings life with him. **99**

Annette de la Renta

66 He's always surrounded by the most attractive people, wonderful friends. There's good food, tennis, golf, swimming and just plain relaxing. **99**

C.Z. Guest

ABOVE: Nan Kempner and Isaac Stern playing Latino in 2000.

LEFT: Pilar Crespi, daughter of Countess Crespi in Santo Domingo, wearing an Oscar de la Renta bathing suit and sarong for a fashion shoot for *Vogue*.

far more seriously, this is where it becomes clear how Oscar de la Renta's philanthropic dedication to the people and economy of his own country has given him the stature of a national father figure. He has U.S. citizenship, but as his home country's official Ambassador-at-Large, he also carries a diplomatic passport from the Dominican Republic. That governmental honor has come to him because of his constant contribution to the support of his people, a commitment that runs far deeper than the froth of fashion.

Oscar's island, nevertheless, is also the place where the sunshine, the color, and the rich heritage of Hispanic culture—not to mention the glamorous women draped at the pool and laughing at dinner— bring the origins of Oscar de la Renta's sensibility into sharp focus. The languid riot of orchid, frangipani, tuberose, oleander, and hibiscus says everything about where his sense of color and pattern originated. Anyone with an eye for design can see how his

romantic native inspiration was nurtured by the sight of the crisp laundered lace, *broderie anglaise*, and gingham worn by Dominican women, and the costumes paraded at religious festivals and weddings. And what more fantastic location could there be for a fashion shoot? Over the years, a cavalcade of beautiful and talented fashion crews has trouped through Oscar's houses and gardens to take photographs for magazines, and has ended up sunbathing, dancing, and being made to feel at home, like everyone else who enters his world. Once again, Oscar de la Renta's work and private life come together to form a seamless continuum.

However, anyone searching for a better understanding of the heart of the man shouldn't start by talking about clothes. Ask him about the Dominican Republic instead: He will fix you with an intense gaze and deliver a passionate lecture about the depth and importance of his country's history. The island of Hispaniola was discovered by Christopher Columbus in 1492. The capital, Santo Domingo, was

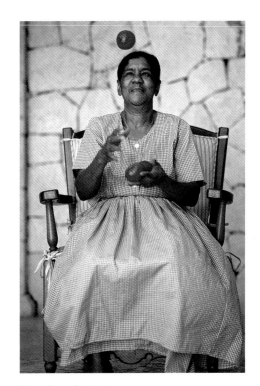

Oscar's cook, Maria.

OPPOSITE: Caribbean trip: Jean Shrimpton in a hot tropical cotton dress that could be now, but dates from 1970.

THIS PAGE: An outside view of Oscar's plantation house at Punta Cana Beach Resort.

Oscar riding on the beach in Santo Domingo with his stepdaughter Eliza Reed Bolen in 1999.

the first city to be founded in the New World, and it was from this jumping-off point that Cortés, Magellan, and Ponce de León began the Spanish conquest of Mexico and Peru in search of gold. Oscar is proud to point out that the Catholic legacy of Santo Domingo means that in any procession of religious dignitaries at the Vatican, the Dominican cardinal precedes all the cardinals of the Americas, because his was the first church in the New World. This matters to him, because Catholicism is an inextricable part of his personality. He worships, with his wife, Annette, and son, Moises, in the simple chapel he had built at his home in Punta Cana, where the local priest says Mass every Sunday.

Punta Cana, on a glorious swath of ocean-fronted land on the southeast coast, is a stupendous symbol of his success. Built from pale, strong, coral rock, solid enough to withstand hurricanes, the house has a façade of eighteen monumental pillars protecting the airy, expansive grace of the high-ceilinged interiors. It's a house designed with the idea of being able to welcome as much family as possible to stay. Here, the refinement of Annette de la Renta's sure hand in interior design is immediately apparent. The colonial structure of the house echoes the early-sixteenth-century mansions built by Spanish grandees—the plantation owners and adventurers. Inside, Annette has assembled treasures (what she calls her "bric-a-brac") accumulated over a lifetime. Eighteenth-century mirrors, classical bookcases, and colonial rattan furniture coexist in easy, English country house harmony with Indian rugs, Chinese vases, and whatever other surprises she feels like pulling down from the attics that week. Close up, the furnishings are saturated with personal memories and associations of a long life spent in the company of an extraordinary society of friends: a needlepoint cushion in a guest bedroom was worked by Slim Keith; an eighteenth-century tinsel picture was a gift from Diana Vreeland; a Jansen chair belonged to decorator Henri Samuel; a 1930s African-inspired screen was a gift from photographer Horst;

The perfect haven. A family place designed for reading, relaxing, quiet, put together by Annette de la Renta, who says "I like to have things around us we've had for years." The mahogany center table in the high-ceilinged drawing room was made by Salvador Gonzalez.

The family next door. Miranda Rijnburger, wearing Oscar de la Renta, playing with her and Julio Iglesias's son Rodrigo in Punta Cana.

A sensitivity to color and texture. The idea of luxury extends from clothes to textiles to furnishings.

OPPOSITE: Guest bedroom in Santo Domingo with an 18th century Spanish mother-of-pearl inlaid secretary.

THIS PAGE: Alek Wek, ultimately chic wearing an embroidered wrap top and mahogany silk skirt for Spring 2001.

and the grandest piece of all, an early-eighteenth-century Spanish secretary, was bought by Oscar on a love-at-first-sight impulse (and paid for in installments over eighteen months), the first expensive piece he ever bought.

Those souvenirs are also silent witnesses to the sounds of laughter, merengue, delicious gossip, and political conversation from an earlier era. Oscar built his first house, the Thai-style Casa de Madera, at Casa de Campo in 1972 with his first wife, Françoise. It was there that the de la Rentas began the holiday house parties, sunshine versions of their New York soirees, in which friends, politicians, and creative people were brought together. Within ten years, the Casa de Campo was a playground for the wealthy, the air buzzing with the sound of private jets shuttling in visitors from the U.S., Spain, and Cuba.

Oscar has been responsible for bestowing a valuable national asset on the Dominican Republic: glamour. It's an aura of gloss that, although intangible, nevertheless contributes to his country's economy through the boost tourism has brought. He's found many other ways of being a more direct benefactor, too. From the beginning, he insisted on employing local craftsmen and cabinetmakers to make the rattan furniture and colonial-style mahogany fixtures and fittings for both Casa de Campo and Punta Cana, thus promoting skills that became so fashionable that guests and neighbors were soon jostling to place their own commissions. None of this, however, compares with the value of the work he has done for the poor children of La Romana in setting up and funding an orphanage and school, La Casa del Niño, and making sure it is sensitively run to mesh with the specific needs of the community.

THIS PAGE: Molten silver halter dress suspended from jeweled rock crystal for the Spring 2001.

OPPOSITE: Candles are lit as nightfalls in the drawing room.

> "His first house at Casa de Campo was influenced by the Philippines and Thailand, with thatched roofs, porches and low eaves, and batiks and hammocks everywhere...it was so influential."

Mica Ertegun

PREVIOUS PAGES LEFT: Angela Lindvall as a romantic heroine in a dress from 2000, shot in Seville, Spain.

PREVIOUS PAGES RIGHT: Oscar's open-air chapel at his home in Santo Domingo, made of coral rock.

THIS PAGE: Guest bedroom with a rattan bed designed by de la Renta that he had made by local craftspeople. The wardrobe is 16th-century Spanish.

It was through his dedication to this project that a life-changing event took place. In 1984, he adopted a boy, Moises, who was ailing until Oscar took him home to nurse him. Oscar became so attached that he could not bear to part with him, and so became a father.

You're always proud to refer to yourself as Latino. What does that mean to you?

I think Latinos in general are very friendly people. There's something about Latin America that's very different from other areas of the world. I can be walking in the street and someone from Venezuela or Ecuador or Peru will recognize me, and they'll say "Oh, Mr. de la Renta, we are so proud of you—you are one of us!" Would you ever hear an Italian telling a Frenchman "I'm so happy you are European like me." There's a very strong sense of brotherhood. We feel a closeness, that we are one. My country has given me a very strong sense of who I am.

From the photos, it's obvious you always have people around you in Santo Domingo. What is it about you and entertaining?

They say extremely intelligent people need to be alone with their thoughts, so I think I must be very stupid—I hate to be on my own! After the collections in March or April, and at Christmas and Thanksgiving, we always have a house full of guests. I am always curious about people and the world. And I've never been a fashion groupie, so my friends come from many spheres. I think I have a sense of diversity in my world that is important.

Your photographs of holidays in Santo Domingo are full of the most incredible people. Even Diana Vreeland, the most powerful woman in New York fashion, is there enjoying herself.

Diana would spend Christmas with us every year, and came even at the very beginning when I had a rented house while we were starting to build our

own. We were in the little town of La Romana, which today is a successful resort. But there was nothing to do there, so it was a big outing for Diana to go to the pharmacy. You can buy almost anything there without a prescription—vitamins to give you youth, and so on. So she and my friend 'Mingo—he was big on that, too—would go to buy Vitamin C by Roche and stuff like that. Every day, more and more people gathered at the pharmacy to see Diana, because they'd never seen anything like her, in her flowing caftan and her hair and all her rouge, and she pretended she didn't know what was going on. Then one day she announced, "Sadly, I have to leave tomorrow!" I said, "Why? Stay longer!" and she replied, "Oh, these people at the pharmacy want more and more, and I have run out of outfits!" It's true—they loved her. They re-baptized it the "Pharmacy Diana."

How did you set up La Casa del Niño?

Like everything else, it started by accident. First of all, I love children. It's the biggest challenge in the world to me to make a child smile. Then, a long time ago a lady came to me to ask if I would pay for the rent of a room to get children off the streets and teach them to read and write. In my country, like in many poor countries all over the world, it is not the tradition in poor communities to marry. It's very common for a man to have two or three sets of children with different women, leaving the mothers behind to care for them. So then the children are sent onto the streets to help the mother with money, running errands in markets, shining shoes, cleaning cars. So I started this little school in one room. But it was difficult to get them to come, because for them it was a waste of time. So I came up with the idea of giving them a meal, and that was a big attraction. So we had a couple of teachers and someone who could cook. Then one day, a very prominent, extraordinary lady, Xiomara Menendez, who is married to a wealthy man in La Romana, knowing I was doing this program and being successful at it, came to me with the idea of setting up an orphanage. I said, "There are so many needs in the area, we cannot really specialize, so how about having somewhere we can meet a lot of needs?" So in 1982, we joined forces and founded Casa del Niño. We take care of 1,200 children on a daily basis who come to school, up to eighth grade, and to a day-care center for newborns upwards, so the mothers can work. We also have programs for blind and deaf-mute children. Xiomara is the one person there on a daily basis. You know, you can always find people who will volunteer to help make a fashion show, but to change diapers on a daily basis—that's different. We employ a lot of people.

So it's not simply an orphanage?

Modern sociologists say that regardless of how extraordinary a place may be for a child, nothing replaces the love of a mother. A child might live in a room with a bare floor, with a bed that goes into the wall, and the mother may be sleeping with three or four children in the bed. And you ask him, would you like to spend the night with us? And he doesn't want to. He wants to go home to his mother.

How do you fund the project?

I do a lot of charity shows, and a lot of my American friends are very generous. People who come to the house always give me checks.

How did you come to adopt Moises?

I always say that Moises and I found each other at a time when we both emotionally needed each other. In 1984, I had just lost my first wife and thought I would never remarry or be a father. He changed my whole life, and I am immensely proud of him.

OPPOSITE: Oscar in his element with children at La Casa del Niño.

FOLLOWING PAGES: Babe Paley and Truman Capote in 1966.

PREVIOUS PAGES LEFT:
The living room of
Oscar's first home, in
Santo Domingo, Casa de
Campo, with rattan fur-
niture made in the
Dominican Republic, in
1988.

PREVIOUS PAGE, RIGHT:
The languid sensuality
of the seventies in a
group of printed peasant
dresses from Early Fall,
1977.

THIS PAGE: Breakfast at
the bungalows in Casa
de Campo.

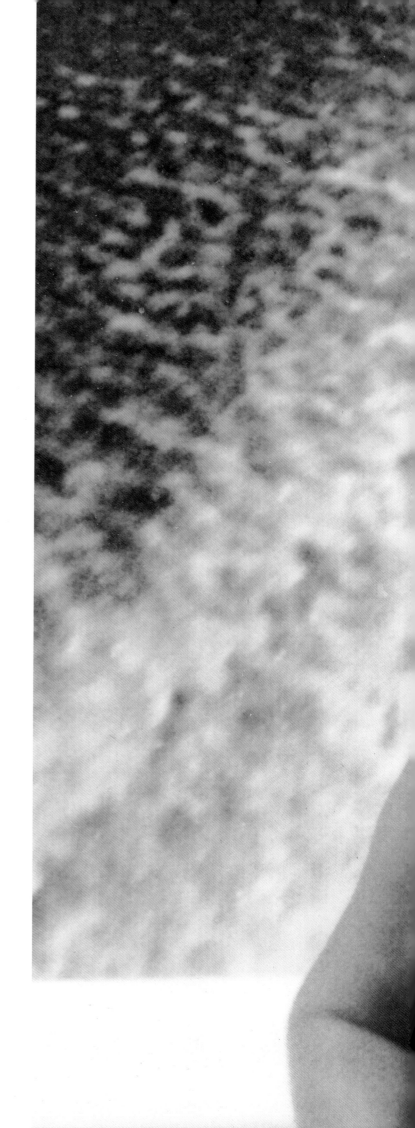

66The greatest
gift Oscar has is
understanding
the lifestyle.
He is surrounded
by and lives with so
many stylish
women, and that
must be a great
source of
inspiration.99

Anna Wintour

Marie-Hélène de Rothschild sunning
herself on boat in the mid-seventies.

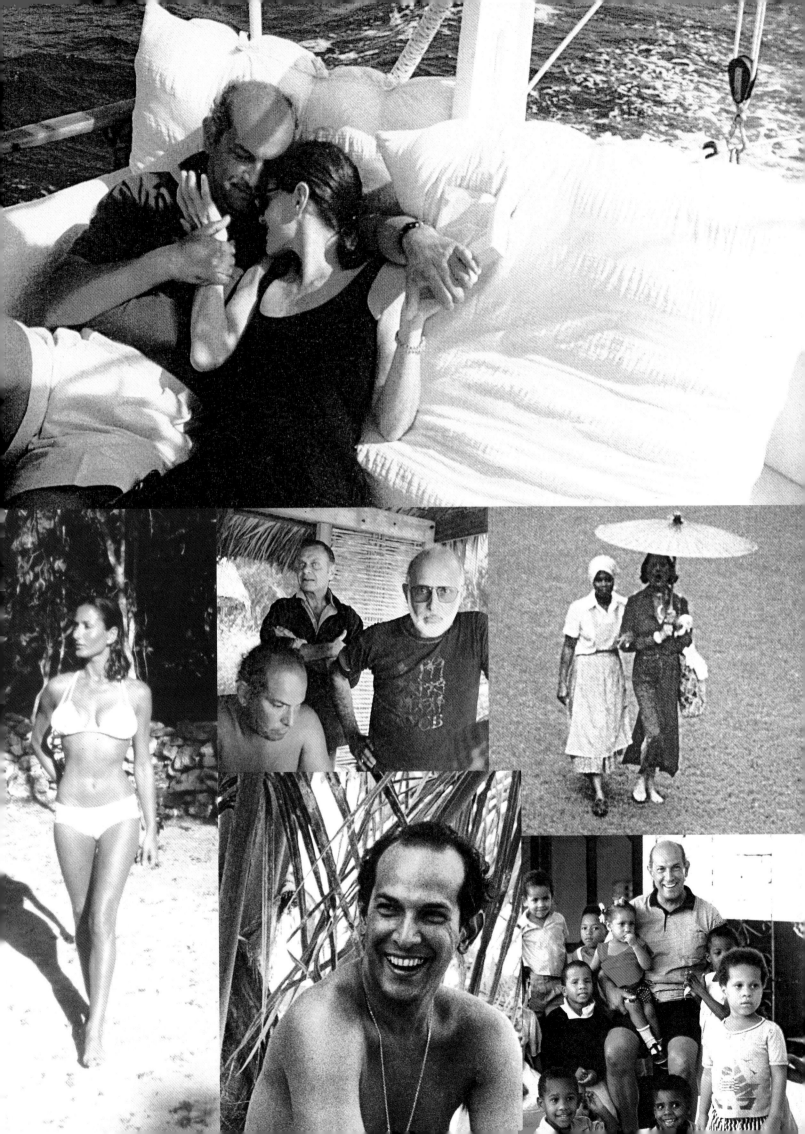

Of all the photographs that have been taken of Oscar and Annette de la Renta, one perhaps symbolizes the most about their relationship, while revealing the least. It's a long-shot, back-view of them strolling together, a dog at Annette's feet, towards their house in Punta Cana. It's not the place, but the gesture that counts. Oscar, towering above his wife, has his arm slung protectively around her tiny shoulders. They are alone, tenderly at ease with one another. You do not see their faces. This image captures something important about their relationship: their closeness, their equilibrium—and the fact that Annette de la Renta, wife of one of the most public personae in American fashion, is an intensely private person. Annette is an elegant, scholarly, and elusive figure who would rather typify herself as a country-woman and a grandmother than accept the praise her friends and admirers give her as an icon of New York elegance.

“ Connecticut is a real private home. Weekdays in New York are crazy, but Connecticut is where Oscar and mum love to garden, surrounded by dogs, chickens. They read, and walk, and watch TV—it's their downtime. ”

Eliza Reed Bolen

annette de la Renta is a patron of the arts who sits on the boards of the Metropolitan Museum of Art, the New York Public Library, the Morgan Library, Rockefeller University, and the Animal Medical Center. Her intellectual interests range from the arts to literature and from medicine to land preservation, while her deepest loves are her four children, six grandchildren, numerous Norfolk terriers, a henhouse full of chickens—and, of course, her adored husband. Between them, Oscar and Annette joke about their differences. Oscar is gregarious; Annette adores being alone. He's mad about music; she likes silence. He loves to go out; she wants to stay in. Oscar jokes that Annette is happiest just to be left alone with her books and her dogs. Yet, somehow, their marriage works beautifully. At their house, Brook Hill Farm, in Kent, in the northwest corner of Connecticut, where they spend an increasing amount of time alone together, an ideal symbolic snapshot of their married happiness would be taken in the garden. Annette would be on her knees weeding, and Oscar would be planting. Above all, they share an intense passion for home.

Annette's first fleeting brush with Oscar de la Renta was as a young girl in the early 1960s, when her mother, Jane Engelhard, herself a beacon of American chic, took her daughter to Elizabeth Arden to see the custom-made clothes the new boy from Paris was designing. Annette's parents, Charles and Jane Engelhard, brought up their five daughters to be cultured and public-spirited. From an early age, following her extraordinary mother, Annette developed a fine eye for great dressing and visual style. Those who know—including top professionals in fashion and interior design—endlessly praise Annette de la Renta as an icon of exemplary contemporary taste. Those who know no better petition her to appear in books and articles on style. She always turns them down.

Though Annette may swear she's more at home in jeans and sweaters, on the rare occasions she's inveigled to appear in public, the figure she cuts at her husband's side is immaculate. A believer in "correct" clothes, she's the kind of woman who has worked out a uniform of simple, sophisticated city separates, consisting of skirt, sweater, and coat. At night, she will probably appear in a long, narrow evening dress, perhaps with a dramatic coat thrown over it, and look radiant—in spite of suffering tortures in the paparazzi glare at public events.

Annette came into Oscar's life as a friend of his first wife, Françoise, in the late 1970s. Annette, then married to Samuel Reed, had three children, Beatrice, Charles, and Eliza. When Françoise died, it was Annette, among other close friends, who rallied to support Oscar. Over a long period, they found their relationship had deepened. Annette divorced, but it was another matter altogether to persuade her it was a good idea to remarry. Oscar, the incorrigible Latin romantic, saw that he would have to take matters into his own hands. Eventually, on the day after Christmas in 1989, they were married in the Dominican Republic with their families around them.

Today, Oscar and Annette divide their time between New York, the Dominican Republic, and Brook Hill Farm in Connecticut, which Oscar bought with Françoise in 1972. The Kent house is very different from the place Oscar discovered thirty years ago.

A passion for nature. Oscar working in the garden in his home in Kent, Connecticut, from an article in French *Elle Décor*, top, and with Annette and dogs in a canoe in the Cascapedia River, bottom.

The garden in Kent is designed by Oscar and Annette to enhance the drama of its wide landscape setting.

Then, it was a humble, ramshackle clapboard house, built in 1935, that he ran across when searching for a weekend retreat near the home of Alexander and Tatiana Liberman. The Libermans had acquired their cottage and forty acres in the 1960s. Oscar fell for the spectacular, rolling grandeur of its setting so thoroughly that he convinced the reluctant Françoise to move there. Françoise's side of the deal was to insist that this house should become their private domain. There would be strict rules about the time Oscar and she would spend alone, and rules about when they could have guests. The long-term vision was that life should be lived well, and that the demands and excitements of the outside world should never be allowed to invade the space of the relationship that matters most.

Those rules—and the monumental mountain views—are the two factors in the de la Renta country household that have remained unchanged from that day to this. Everything else has been altered. Inside, Annette and Oscar have improved the house by adding a large bedroom, but it's the outside that they have enjoyed working on most. More acres have been bought to preserve their isolation, and the garden, initially designed by Russell Page, has matured into one of the most stunningly elegant private sanctuaries in America.

Oscar and Annette devote themselves to tending and extending that garden with the fervor of true horticultural enthusiasts. This quiet side of Oscar's interests is something his city clientele may never guess—though neither would they necessarily identify with his passion for classical music, nor his love of simple good food and enjoying the sunrise. Yet this down-to-earth side of his character—and the love of a good woman—makes Oscar de la Renta a bigger and more complete man. As his friend C.Z. Guest puts it, "Oscar is a rounded person. He has a big view."

Box hedges form an alley in one of Oscar's garden "rooms" in Connecticut.

ABOVE: Gardening with Moises.

OPPOSITE: Oscar at home in the country with Moises, Annette, Annette's son, Charlie, Annette's daughters Beatrice Niven and Eliza, and Beatrice's three children, Charlie, Nicky, and Katherine.

Annette is a woman of great character and discipline, but also enigmatically private. What are the qualities that drew you to her?

First, Annette is very beautiful. Second, she has an unbelievable brain—and a highly irreverent sense of humor to go with it. Third, she has extraordinary taste, better than any decorator I know. Fourth, she is incredibly loving and kind. Annette gave Moises and me an extended family: first and foremost her three wonderful children, Eliza, Beatrice, and Charles, and her four brilliant and loving sisters, Susan, Sophie, Sally, and Charlene. Annette and I were friends first, and then I fell madly in love with her. I thought she would never marry me, but she did!

Your house in Kent has been a life's work. Why did you want to live in that part of the country?

I think when you live in a city like New York, it's wonderful—essential, even—to be able to get

away. Françoise and I were very influenced by the Libermans, who we would visit for weekends in Connecticut. We strongly wanted a different, casual pace of life. A lot of people we knew were buying houses in the Hamptons. But life in Southampton has the same social demands as the city—there are dinners and luncheons every Saturday and Sunday. In Kent, it is true country life.

When you bought the house, Françoise had stipulations. What were they?

She agreed to buy the house on two conditions. First, that if we had guests, they would come on Saturday and leave on Sunday after lunch. Second, that we would always arrive on Friday afternoon and leave on Monday, so that we would always have two nights together alone. It was very important for our marriage, and is even more so for my marriage to Annette. She's not a party person. She's an outdoor person. She loves quiet, dogs, the garden.

Oscar's barn in Kent.

LEFT: Naomi Campbell in a city girl's neat wool suit from 1996.

OPPOSITE: Tulip time at Oscar's garden in Kent.

Garden pathway. Red Spire pear trees frame one of the many garden sculptures.

Though you are such a public figure, your private life, the time you devote to it, and how you live it is vital to you. Why do you think that is?

I'm a Cancer. A homemaker. Both with Françoise and Annette, it has been very important to me to spend a lot of time in the home. I'm much more a builder than a decorator—an architect manqué. Annette is the decorator, as was Françoise. Before I married, I never had a proper home. To me, home is wherever Annette is.

Annette was happy to take on the house and your way of life there?

When we married, Annette already owned a beautiful Federal-style house at Katonah, New York. Our Kent house does not compare in any way architecturally. Ideally, Annette would rather have torn it down and started again. But what we have there is an immense hilltop view stretching for miles. She decided that the situation, scale, and potential of the garden in Kent was much greater, so when we started our life together she decided to sell her house and concentrate on what we could do here. Making the garden has taken many years, and Annette never stops. She will go out and spend hours on her knees, weeding. She'll even weed with a flashlight in the dark—though now it's land clearance and planting trees that preoccupies her most.

Tell me about how your passion for gardening began.

Though I have loved nature since my childhood, I never thought—perhaps because I have always lived in cities—that one day I would have a garden of my own. When Françoise and I arrived at Brook Hill Farm, neither of the previous owners had thought of making a garden, probably because of the natural physical beauty of the place. But I started thinking about it and had the idea of inviting the great gardener Russell Page to come and visit for the weekend. At that time, Françoise and I had an apartment on East 70th Street, overlooking the Frick Museum, and I'd watched Russell creating the garden there. So I took him around our property, and when we came to the terrace, I was totally dismayed when he asked me, "What is it you want to have?" "A garden," I replied. "You will never have a garden," he said, "because a garden is a room and to have a room you need walls and you have none. The eye stops at the horizon; the only thing you could do here is add more trees to frame the view." A few weeks before his visit, I'd bought a book from the White Flower Farm and had been preparing and planting a herbaceous border in a half-moon shape. I was all excited in anticipation of Russell's reaction. In the most polite but icy manner, he looked down at it as we passed by and asked, "What is that?" I was so utterly embarrassed, I said it was there when I bought the house! After that, Russell made a plan for me. From that visit on, I have built nothing but walls!

Spectacularly graceful. Eliza Reed Bolen, Aerin Lauder and Marina Rust, dressed in Oscar's liquid evening dresses, watch his friend Mikhail Baryshnikov swan dive into the pool in Kent.

Could you explain the concept of your garden "rooms"?

First, I planted a wall of yew around our pool—this eventually became our very first "room," where I have only white flowers of late bloom so that the garden is in flower at the time the pool is in use. The second room is what used to be a parking area, and the third—my favorite—is what I call my "secret garden," which was originally intended as a rose garden. It was built in a space 50 feet by 50 feet and simply divided into four planting areas by a brick path. It's a paradise.

But gardening is more than a horticultural exercise. Do you and Annette find a deeper dimension in it?

A garden is probably the most spiritual and pure of joys. It's a communion with nature and beauty in the most simple and fundamental form. It is an experience that needs to be lived at every instant. In a garden, one cannot reflect on something bad. What is truly wonderful is that it teaches you a lesson about life's continuity. In a sense, a garden is a fragile vision that can quickly disappear out of neglect, but with constant work and tender love, it can preserve beauty forever.

The long gallery in Oscar's New York apartment contains the library, the sitting room and a dining area, 1992.

Bridget Foley in *W* magazine, November 2001, captured it all: Oscar de la Renta, she wrote, "presides actively over a thirty-six-year-old fashion house that is more vibrant than it has ever been." Remarkably, since the mid-1990s, business has surged, a new generation of beautiful women has flocked to his clothes, and Oscar is more energized by his work than ever. A head count of the slim, soigné people who choose to run around in Oscar's dresses now reads like a list of the active, go-getting, and talented of America: Sarah Jessica Parker, Aerin Lauder Zinterhofer, Princess Marie-Chantal of Greece, Lauren du Pont, Marina Rust, Brooke de Ocampo, Cate Blanchett. Is there any other living designer who has captured the hearts of two successive generations the way Oscar has? Has anyone else, with such quietly effective aplomb, managed to change his business and move with the times—and yet still stay true to his own vision?

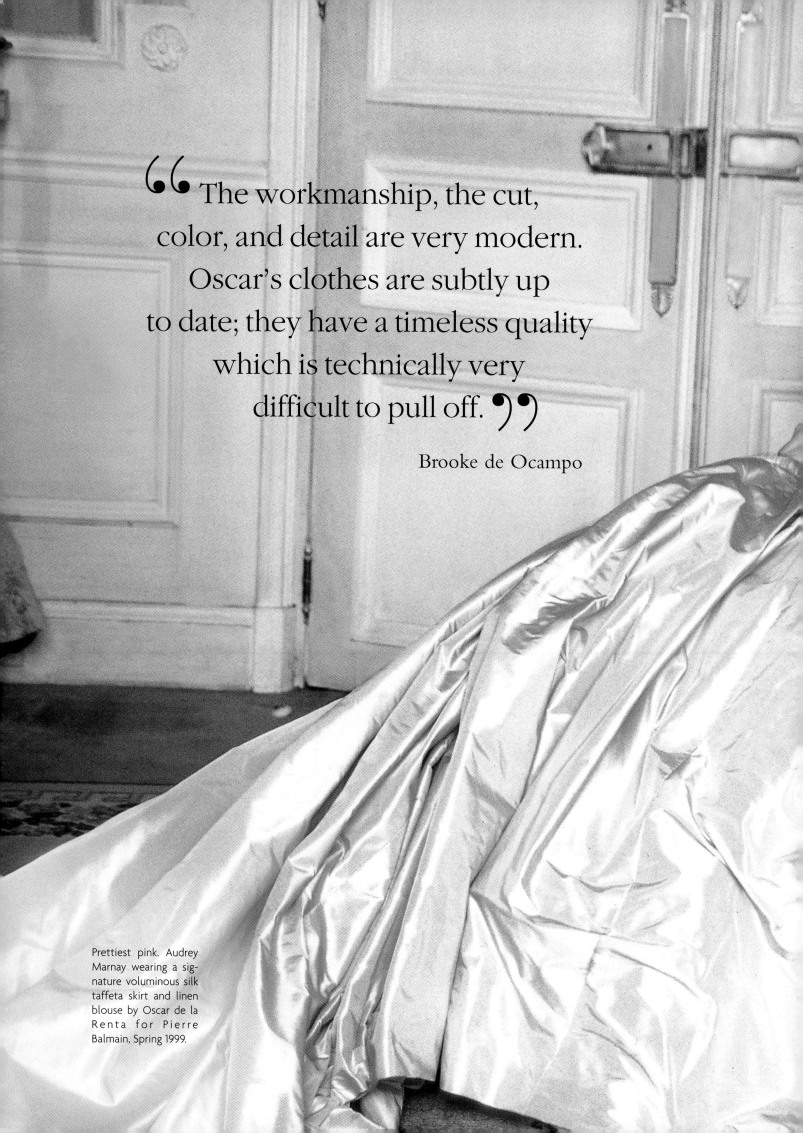

"The workmanship, the cut, color, and detail are very modern. Oscar's clothes are subtly up to date; they have a timeless quality which is technically very difficult to pull off."

Brooke de Ocampo

Prettiest pink. Audrey Marnay wearing a signature voluminous silk taffeta skirt and linen blouse by Oscar de la Renta for Pierre Balmain, Spring 1999.

C ompare the lithe dresses and neat separates Oscar de la Renta designs now with the gowns and daywear he created in the 1960s, and the differences are less striking than the similarities. Today, the silhouettes may be simpler—strapless and slim, maybe, rather than stately and grand—but still, there's the lace, the color, the tulle, the fairy-dust sprinkle of bead, and of course, always, somewhere, the ruffle. More than that, what counts above all is the aura of romantic femininity that surrounds the girl who is wearing Oscar de la Renta. What you see, as much as the dress, is the dream that enfolds her.

Even in the tough twenty-first century, it turns out that independent, achieving, time-pressed women of the world still love to look ravishingly, delicately feminine when the occasion calls. Almost everything may have changed about the lives they lead compared to their mothers, but the thread of that fantasy is unbroken, generation to generation. Understanding that is as much Oscar de la Renta's secret today as it was in 1965. The difference now is that he can pull today's girl together in a total look, from the dainty little bag dangling from her wrist to the bejeweled tip of her satin toe, while her mother—also a modern person, these days—delights in dressing exactly the same way. Finally, the Oscar de la Renta picture is complete—not young, nor old, but timeless. And business is booming.

None of this, however, has come about by the waving of some magic wand. Just when other designers might be resting on the laurels of a long career, Oscar de la Renta went at it all over again, with no letup. Never complacent and always voraciously curious about the world at large, he saw how times had changed and deliberately set out on a campaign to woo a glamorous new clientele. Behind the scenes, that meant continuing the structural changes that had already begun to happen as far back as 1987, when a contract lawyer, Jeffry Aronsson, was hired as outside counsel by Oscar to help with the detail of a licensing deal. Aronsson proved to be a deft negotiator and gradually gained Oscar's trust. In 1995, he arranged an amicable ending to the business partnership between the designer and the manufacturer Gerald Shaw, son of Benjamin Shaw, his original backer. Aronsson was then appointed president and chief executive officer, becoming part of the new team that led Oscar de la Renta's business to undergo its remarkable renaissance.

Cleverly, Oscar began to bring young people into the business, knowing that an influx of new blood would be a better way to rev things up than any amount of second-hand market research. Oscar's stepdaughter, Eliza Reed Bolen, went to work in the licensing department and has ended up doing a thorough housecleaning, dividing the Oscar de la Renta label into two coherent lines: Oscar by Oscar de la Renta is positioned as bridge product; Oscar de la Renta is the signature for the luxe, upscale output of the house. Adam Lippes joined as creative director and Alexandra Hamilton as head of public relations. Within a couple of years, by the late 1990s, Oscar had surrounded himself with a gang of dynamic, talented people who were mostly under the age of thirty. As the American economy began booming, word went around that something was happening at

OPPOSITE: A quintessential haute couture moment, caught backstage at Pierre Balmain show in Paris, Fall 2001.

NEXT PAGES: Christy Turlington wearing a silk charmeuse dress for Oscar de la Renta, Spring 2001.

THIS PAGE: Girls will be girls. Sisters Tamzin and Arabella Greenhill live out the modern Oscar fantasy in silk satin gowns from Fall 1998.

OPPOSITE: Snaps and souvenirs. Bulletin board in Oscar's New York studio, 1989.

Oscar with supermodels Christy Turlington, Linda Evangelista and Claudia Schiffer, Winter 1992.

Oscar's studio. He was open to every piece of new evidence his team brought him about the way young women want to dress. At every charity event he chaired, every opening, wedding, lunch, and movie he went to, he watched how young women were dressing with a new-pared down simplicity—but how, also, the current image was glossy, considered, and radiantly glamorous. And with his couture-learned skills and lifelong adulation of femininity, Oscar de la Renta was precisely the man to know how to do that.

The result: the de la Renta grand-entrance ball gowns of the 1980s melted into the body-flattering evening dresses of the 1990s. He began recalibrating the collection to contain pieces that could span multiple needs in a modern woman's breakneck schedule—gorgeous tops that can do evening but will also look hip with jeans by day, and pretty sweater sets that are great for dinner and just as right for doing a business deal. He also rethought the jacket-and-skirt suit that had once been the uniform of the Ladies Who Lunch (and a significant element of his success in the 1980s), offering different, looser options for a chic busy day, such as matching coordinates of coat, skirt, pants, and perhaps sweater. All of this could be done oh-so-subtly, without changing any of the characteristic design traits he was known for, or losing an older clientele while gaining the new.

In this whole modernization process, one other thing never changed. All along, Oscar's talent for understanding social appropriateness has allowed him to match clothes to the reality of the customer's psychology and roles, knowing exactly where she was going to wear his things and how they must perform for her. In 2000, onlookers among Oscar's peer group registered their admiration for his design relevance, when he was voted Womenswear Designer of the Year by the CFDA.

Oscar, Jeffry, and the rest of the team were also busy, completing licensing deals and brainstorming future strategy. The essential idea they isolated was the concept that had kept Oscar relevant all along: "timeless topicality," they call it. Next, they planned two key objectives: high-end accessories, and launching freestanding stores. Everything labeled with the "Oscar de la Renta" mark would follow the inspiration and style of

Oscar's understanding of clothes for American occasions, and the women who wear them, is a constant currency whatever the decade.

ABOVE: A model presents for a "salmon" ensemble by Oscar de la Renta for Pierre Balmain, Spring 2001.

RIGHT: Annette going to the Metropolitan Opera wearing an Oscar de la Renta peacock blue satin cape, in 2001.

Town&Country

ESTABLISHED IN 1860

WELCOME
BACK
ELEGANCE!
PRETTY CLOTHES
TOP TRENDS
GLAMOROUS
ACCESSORIES
**WELL-SUITED
MEN**
LUSTROUS
PEARLS

**FALL
FASHION**
SPECIAL ISSUE

SEPTEMBER 2000
U.S. $4.00 CANADA $5.00
FOREIGN $5.00

TOWN&COUNTRY

MAY 1993

DE LA RENTA
Reshapes Fashion

JUNIOR LEAGUE
Takes Off Its White Gloves

ROYAL TOIL
A Windsor Who Works!

STORK CLUBS
A Guide to Adoption

REVISTA

DISEÑADORES

JUAN CARLOS | navarro

CUANDO SE DEFINE DICE SER SOLIDARIO CON EL DOLOR, MAS
QUE NADA, DE LOS NIÑOS. POR ELLOS, PRECISAMENTE, HA HECHO
MUCHAS COSAS. NO HABLAREMOS DE ESO. LO HAREMOS, BASICA-
MENTE, SOBRE LOS DETALLES DE SU VIDA.

OSCAR
DE LA RENTA solidario con el dolor humano

VOGUE
*celebrates
american fashion*

Rich in detail,
dramatic in
dimension, his
famously
glamorous
eveningwear
exudes
Park Avenue
elegance.
Photographed by
Arthur Elgort.

oscar
de la renta

DICKSON'S NEW DREAM/2   PENNEY'S $200M AD BLITZ/39

WWD MONDAY
Accessories/Innerwear

**Ballet
Class**

LOS ANGELES

AND THE OSCAR

GO... TO ...BALMAIN

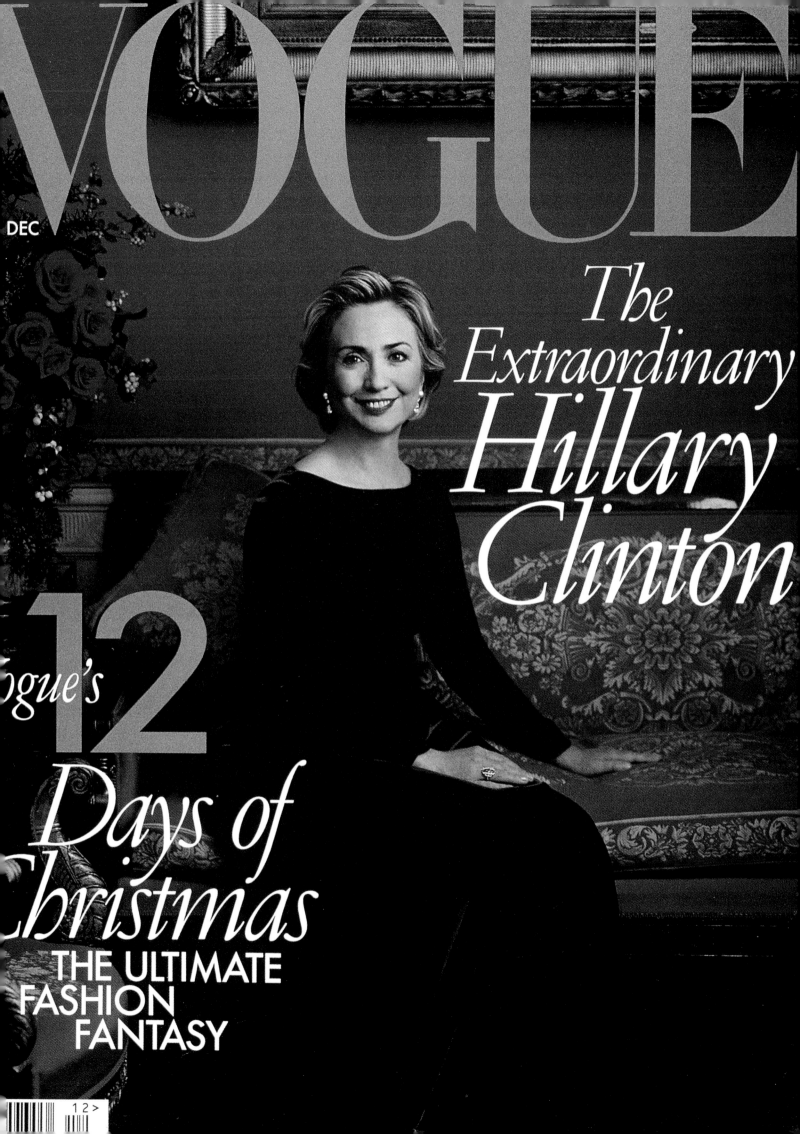

VOGUE

DEC

The *Extraordinary* **Hillary Clinton**

12

ogue's

Days of Christmas

THE ULTIMATE FASHION FANTASY

PREVIOUS PAGES RIGHT: Hillary Clinton wears Oscar de la Renta for the cover of the December 2001 issue of *Vogue* magazine—it was the first time a First Lady appeared on the cover of the magazine.

THIS PAGE: The house revolves around Oscar's inspiration, the energy of his young team, and the enthusiasm of a whole new generation of pace-setting customers like Sarah Jessica Parker of *Sex and the City*, who wears a white organza flamenco dress from Spring 2002.

Oscar's personal culture, always exuding a sense of true luxury, beautiful handcraft, and integrity. In February 2001 came the launch of Oscar's ravishingly decorative shoes and bags, all saturated in details—embroidery, needlepoint, fur trim, jewels. These flowed from and complemented his collection. In the same year came another milestone: the opening of a store-in-store boutique at Bergdorf Goodman, a domain decorated in homage to Oscar's plantation-style house in the Dominican Republic, with coral and mahogany in a sunny atmosphere of chic gaiety. It's a blueprint, in miniature, of the full-fledged stores that are on the business drawing board, a centerpiece of Oscar's design for the future.

What keeps you inspired and so energetic?

One of the greatest assets a human being can have is curiosity. Still, today, the best time is when I am working with the collection. It's a very fast business, and there are so many young people here. The fact that everyone in my studio is so young makes it more exciting. I depend on people. To me, the creative process is teamwork. I always joke about making my assistants mad, because if a cleaning man happens to be in the studio when I am fitting a dress, I ask him what he thinks about it. I like a reaction! There's always an emotional sense to what you are doing. In my studio, at the end of designing the collection, when we are putting it together, photographing it, and putting it on the wall before the day of the show, we have a tradition that everyone has to write down what we like and what we hate. I always like what nobody else likes. You are so emotionally involved. I know deep down that they are right—but I feel sorry for the dress!

What is your customer like now?

My clothes today are again so well accepted. My clothes have always been the essence of femininity. Today, being a woman is wonderful. To express femininity is great. I always say the woman I dressed in the sixties is on the list of endangered species—because that

PREVIOUS PAGE: Oscar's early fascination for Russian riches revisted for Balmain haute couture for Fall, 1997.

LEFT: The youth vote. A new generation has flocked to be dressed by Oscar. Carmen Kass, left, channels the energy of femininity in a gold lace blouse and taffeta skirt, Fall 2001.

ABOVE: Oscar's return to Paris for his first Pierre Balmain couture show, 1993.

OPPOSITE: British pop star Victoria Beckham opts for opulence in Oscar's cerise taffeta gown for a *Vogue* portrait with her husband David, Spring 1999.

66 Oscar completely understands who he is and who he is dressing. . .He's never tried to be avant-garde or difficult. He just does really good uptown clothes, never overtly sexy but attractive, colorful and feminine. 99

Anna Wintour

woman who used to go to lunch and whose husband paid all the bills doesn't exist any more. There is this emergence of the professional, working woman who is in total control of her destiny. A deep knowledge of who the consumer is and keeping abreast of change is vital. And the task has been to keep it young and fresh and, at the same time, my point of view.

How have you changed your business?

After I married Annette, my life changed a lot, and then Eliza came to work with me, and Jeffry Aronsson became my president and CEO in 1994. There's been an influx of young people into my company, and into the whole image of the clothes. That started all the changes in my business, and I began feeling more ambitious about my work, and more competitive than I was. I feel it's great: we need to renew ourselves to stay in business.

How did it feel to win the CFDA Womenswear Designer of the Year award in 2000?

One of the most important things to me in fashion is staying power. I probably have more accolades and better reviews now than I ever have. I really believe the last ten years have been the most important in my career. When I look back at my first collections, I see how uneven they were, the tension between trying to exert my fantasies and trying to be commercial and sell at the same time. What I have learned is to be a better editor of myself. Today, I think it is sad that young designers can become famous in the press overnight and the following season are out of business. With me, I was making clothes, they were selling in the stores; it came over a period of time.

In the middle of the renaissance of your own label, you were invited to become the couturier at Pierre Balmain in Paris in 1993. What tempted you to do it?

I really started my career in haute couture, and when I was offered it, I was honored. I was and am the only American designer in Paris doing haute couture. When I joined Balmain in 1993, they hadn't sold a single couture dress in two years. I wanted to give it back a sense of credibility, in the sense of what couture used to be. It was a very different scene in the nineties than it was in the sixties. Balmain once employed 800 people, and now there are a maximum of forty-five working on the couture. So there had to be a new relevance, something a woman with a certain lifestyle could relate to. Especially with American customers, daywear is really a skirt, pants, and sweater—so evening wear is really the emphasis on something custom-made. Now Pierre Balmain is among the houses that sell the most dresses in Paris.

What distinguishes a couture dress from ready-to-wear?

From the creative point of view, there are no limits in couture. You are exercising your talent and fantasy without any holding back. But there is still a consideration in my mind. Unfortunately, success is not what fashion editors like: that is something that comes when an anonymous woman in the street wants to wear it.

The elegance of Oscar's way with lace is a constantly updated design obsession, here executed in the ultimate modern deluxe manner using laser-etched flowers on black, for Pierre Balmain, modeled by Amber Valletta.

Symbolically, you have dedicated your new fragrance, "Intrusion," to this new woman?

For years and years, it was a man's world—and now, suddenly, someone else arrives on the scene: the modern woman in charge of her life and destiny. The advertising image is shot by Ines van Lamsweerde and Vinoodh Matadin, showing a Mexican girl, Liliana Dominguez, who has a strong, beautiful face, and is wearing a simple black lace dress of mine. She looks powerful, elegant, confident, and sensual all at the same time.

It's obvious you still get a huge kick out of designing and tracking how women are changing.

People are always asking me which decade I'd choose as the best to be designing in. I always say, "Now!" There has never been a more interesting time than the present. The twenty-first century is the century of the woman: never before in history has a woman been more in charge of her own destiny. I feel lucky to be dressing the most interesting women there have ever been.

Finally, Oscar, what gives you the most satisfaction from your life and work?

Above all, the people I love. And to try to have a life that is well lived. Every day I wake and see the sunrise, I look up and say, "God, thank you."

PREVIOUS PAGES: Oscar de la Renta's sense of drama plays to a whole new generation of young achievers. Here, Kate Moss strikes a diva stance in a sculpted ivory silk dress and feathered coat for Pierre Balmain, Fall 1999, watched by Sean "Puffy" Combs.

LEFT: Grand finale. In his element, surrounded by a tribe of beautiful women in gold-spun lace, Oscar de la Renta takes a final bow at his Spring show in 1996.

BIOGRAPHY

Oscar de la Renta was born on July 22, 1932, in Santo Domingo, and left his native Dominican Republic at eighteen years of age to study painting in Madrid. He entered the Real Academia de Bellas Artes de San Fernando in 1951. While living in Spain, he discovered his talents for fashion and began sketching for leading Spanish fashion houses, which soon led to an apprenticeship with Spain's most renowned couturier, Cristobal Balenciaga.

In 1961, Oscar de la Renta left Spain to join Antonio Castillo as a couture assistant at the house of Lanvin in Paris. In 1963, he came to New York to design the couture collection for Elizabeth Arden and in 1965, joined Jane Derby and began his own signature ready-to-wear label.

Over the past thirty-five years, this label has grown to include an important collection of clothing and accessories based on his signature style. Oscar de la Renta's collections for women include his "Signature Collection," "Pink Label," and "Oscar by Oscar de la Renta." The Oscar de la Renta menswear line comprises formal wear, suits, sportscoats, trousers, and a full range of furnishings. Throughout Latin America, there is a popular sportswear line for men and boys, "Oscar," a jeans collection for men and women, "Oscar Jeans," and a women's lifestyle collection, "O by Oscar de la Renta."

Oscar de la Renta launched his first perfume for women, "Oscar," in 1977. Today, it is a best-selling perfume in over seventy countries and winner of the 1991 Fragrance Foundation Perennial Success Award. In 1980, Oscar created a fragrance for men, "Pour Lui," reflecting the man of style and confidence. In 1992, "Volupté" was introduced as a contemporary classic. In 1995, he was the recipient of the Living Legend Award from the American Society of Perfumes. Oscar launched a new fragrance for women, "SO de la Renta," in the fall of 1997. A sheer luscious floral, this scent was created for the woman with an independent attitude and effortless sense of style. In the fall of 1999, "Oscar for Men" debuted. The fragrance line now includes a home collection, "Oscar Home," in three distinctive scents: "City," "Island," and "Country." In April 2002, he launched a new perfume called "Intrusion."

Oscar de la Renta's talents have received widespread international recognition. In 1970, he was honored by the President of the Dominican Republic. Among many other honors, Mr. de la Renta is a two-time winner of the Coty American Fashion Critic's Award (in 1967 for the "Russian Look" and in 1968 for the "Belle Epoque Look") and was inducted into the Coty Hall of Fame in 1973. From 1973 to 1976 and from 1986 to 1988, he served as President of the Council of Fashion Designers of America (CFDA). In February 1990, this organization honored him with the CFDA Lifetime Achievement Award.

With his Spring 1993 collection for the house of Pierre Balmain Haute Couture, Paris (for which he began designing in 1992), Oscar de la Renta became the first American to design for a French couture house. In 1996, Mr. de la Renta received the Lifetime Achievement Award from the Hispanic Heritage Society. In 2000, Oscar received the CFDA (Council of Fashion Designers of America) Womenswear Designer of the Year award and he was recently awarded the France's Legion d'Honneur as a Commandeur, as well as the Gold Medal of Fine Arts from the King of Spain.

In the Dominican Republic, Oscar de la Renta's influence has reached beyond fashion. He has helped build two much-needed schools incorporating orphanages and day-care centers in La Romana and Punta Cana. The 1,500 children attending these schools come from a variety of disadvantaged backgrounds. Proper meals, medical and dental facilities and a loving, caring staff contribute to the health and well-being of the children. There are also special classes for the deaf and mute, as well as for the blind. The aim of these schools is not to take the children away from their families, but to strengthen the familial ties by aiding in times and areas of need. For his endless work in the Dominican Republic, Oscar has been awarded with the order of Merito de Juan Pablo Duarte, as well as the order of Cristobal Colon.

In the United States, Oscar de la Renta is a tireless patron of the arts. He serves on the boards of The Metropolitan Opera, Carnegie Hall and Thirteen/WNET. He is also on the board of important cultural institutions such as The Americas Society and The Spanish Institute. In 2000, Mr. de la Renta had the honor of serving as Grand Marshall of New York City's Hispanic Day Parade.

Oscar de la Renta has never been far from his native Dominican Republic. After twenty-eight years in Casa de Campo, a once-sleepy resort town that over time has evolved into a crowded destination for the international jet set, the de la Rentas moved their home to Punta Cana on the eastern coast of the Dominican Republic. Oscar has become involved in the 400-room Punta Cana Beach Resort located on 15,000 acres of pristine land. In addition to developing the resort, preserving the majority of the land as an ecological reserve has become one of Oscar's top priorities.

Just as the Dominican Republic is in Oscar's blood, so it is in his designs. He thrives on the sun, warmth, and strong, clean colors associated with his homeland. He is both rejuvenated and inspired when he returns home. Nonetheless, Oscar is passionate about traveling and finds it a source of great inspiration, which is often reflected in the exotic elegance of many of his collections.

PHOTOGRAPHIC CREDITS

8-11: © Oscar de la Renta archives

14-15: Bertrand Rieger/Hémisphères

16-17: Oscar de la Renta archives

18: © Time Pix

20: © John Huba/A+C Anthology/*Town & Country*

20: © Assouline Publishing

21: © Assouline Publishing

21: © Time Pix

22: © Pascal Rossignol © Reuters /CORBIS

23: © Carter Smith/A+C Anthology/*W* Magazine

24: © Carlo Pieroni/Korman+Company

24-25 center: © Oscar de la Renta archives

24-25 center: © Oscar de la Renta archives

25: © Assouline Publishing

26: © Oscar de la Renta archives

27: © John Casado

28: Henry Clarke/ © *Vogue*, Condé Nast

29: © Lipnitzki-Viollet

30: bottom left: © Maria Valentino/MCV Photo

30: top right: © Oscar de la Renta archives

31: © Oscar de la Renta archives

32: © Ellen von Unwerth/A+C Anthology

33: Irving Penn © 1970 (renewed 1998) Condé Nast

34: © Oscar de la Renta archives

35: © Steven Meisel/A+C Anthology/ © *Vogue*, Condé Nast

36-37: © Antonio/Oscar de la Renta archives

38: © Craig McDean/ A+C Anthology/ *Harper's Bazaar*

41: Raymundo de Larrain/ © *Vogue*, Condé Nast

42: © Oscar de la Renta archives

47: © Oscar de la Renta archives

47: © Oscar de la Renta archives

48: © Oscar de la Renta archives

50: © *Women's Wear Daily*

51 top left: © Oscar de la Renta archives

52 top right: © Oscar de la Renta archives

51 bottom right: © Oscar de la Renta archives

52: © Oscar de la Renta archives

53: Bert Stern/ © *Vogue*, Condé Nast

54: © Oscar de la Renta archives

55: © Oscar de la Renta archives

56 bottom left: © Oscar de la Renta archives

56 top right: © Oscar de la Renta archives

57: © Oscar de la Renta archives

59: Irving Penn/© 1967 (renewed 1996) *Vogue*, Condé Nast

60: top left: © Harry Benson/Archive Films

60: center right: © Oscar de la Renta archives

61: © Oscar de la Renta archives

62: © Oscar de la Renta archives

65: Arnaud de Rosnay/ © *Vogue*, Condé Nast

67: ©Neal Barr/Collection Library Metropolitan Museum of Art, New York

68 top left: Ichiro Fujimura/ © *WWD*

68 center left: Richard Avedon/ © *Vogue*, Condé Nast

68 bottom middle: © Courtesy of *Harpers Bazaar*

68 right: © *Cue*

68 bottom left: Richard Avedon/ © *Vogue*, Condé Nast

68 bottom right: Horst/ © *Vogue*, Condé Nast

69: © Eric Boman/ *New York Times Magazine*

70: © Oscar de la Renta archives

72: Irving Penn ©/ 1969 (renewed 1997) Condé Nast

73: Irving Penn ©/ 1967 (renewed 1995) Condé Nast

75 top left: © Oscar de la Renta archives

75 top right: © Oscar de la Renta archives

75 center left: © Oscar de la Renta archives

75: center right: © Owen Franken/CORBIS

75 bottom: © Oscar de la Renta archives

76: Henry Clarke/ © *Vogue*, Condé Nast

77 top left: Patrick Demarchelier/ © *Vogue*, Condé Nast

77 top right: Patrick Demarchelier/ © *Vogue*, Condé Nast

77 center left: Toscani/ © *Vogue*, Condé Nast

77 center right: © *Hola*

77 bottom left: © John Huba/ Courtesy of *Town & Country*

77 bottom center: Thomas Iannacone/ © *WWD*

77 bottom right: © Gilles Bensimon/ *Elle*

78: © Oscar de la Renta archives

80 top left: © Oscar de la Renta archives

80 right: © Oscar de la Renta archives

81: Bert Stern/ © *Vogue*, Condé Nast Publications Inc.

82: © Oscar de la Renta archives

83: Irving Penn/ © 1968 (renewed 1995) Condé Nast

84: Tony Palmieri/ © *WWD*

85: Arnaud de Rosnay/ © *Vogue*, Condé Nast

86: © Oscar de la Renta archives

87: Gianni Penati/ © *Vogue*, Condé Nast

88 top left: Reginald Gray/ © *WWD*

88 top right: Mark Ellidge/ © *Vogue*, Condé Nast

88 center left: Mark Ellidge/ © *Vogue*, Condé Nast

88 center middle: © Helmut Newton/ *Vogue*, Condé Nast

88 center right: Reginald Gray/ © *WWD*

88 bottom left: Mark Ellidge/ © *Vogue*, Condé Nast

88 bottom right: Reginald Gray/ © *WWD*

91: Bert Stern/ © *Vogue*, Condé Nast

ACKNOWLEDGMENTS

Oscar de la Renta would like to thank *Vogue* magazine and Condé Nast publications and all of the photographers who participated in the book, especially Arthur Elgort, Richard Felber, Oberto Gili, François Halard, Annie Leibovitz, Irving Penn and Mario Testino. He also thanks Barbara Black, Eliza Reed Bolen, Mica Ertegun, John Fairchild, C.Z. Guest, Nancy Kissinger, Aerin Lauder, Brooke de Ocampo, and Barbara Walters for their words.

Mr. de la Renta would especially like to thank Anna Wintour for her support, and most of all, his family and his wife, Annette for allowing infringement on her privacy.

The publisher would like to thank Michel Arnaud, Richard Avedon, Quentin Bacon, Bernstein Andriulli, Jennifer Bikel at Fairchild Publications, Eric Boman, Judy Casey, Chris Boals Artists, Michael Stier and Leigh Montville at Condé Nast, Wendelien Daan, Noe DeWitt, Kathleen Hopkins at Time Pix, Jacques Dirand, Odile Fraignault at Lanvin Castillo, Inside Photo, Kanji Ishii, Kramer & Kramer, Peter Lindbergh and The Lighthouse, Roxanne Lowit, Magnum Photos, Candice Marks at Art Partner, Neiman Marcus, Jessica Miranda at Jed Root, MCV Photo, Patricia Muzikar at Korman and Company, Amy Neunsinger, Michelle Ocampo at Arthur Elgort Studio, Gladys Perint Palmer, Jennifer Palmer at Art and Commerce, David Hans Plotkin at Corbis, Claire Powell, Saks Fifth Avenue, Jefferey Smith at Contact Press, Solve Sundsbo, Chantal Vizioz at Balmain, Barbara Von Schreiber at I2I, and Valerie Zars at Getty Images.

And to all the publications who participated: *Harper's Bazaar, House & Garden, Elle, Hola, In Style, Marie Claire, The New York Times, Town & Country, Travel & Leisure, Vanity Fair,* W, and *Women's Wear Daily*.

We would also like to thank all the models, model agencies, and actors who allowed their images to be used, and the entire staff at Oscar de la Renta for all their help and support in making this book.

A note from the publisher: extensive efforts were undertaken to identify the owners of all rights; errors or omissions brought to the attention of the publisher will be corrected at the time of the next edition.